Essential Histories

The Crusades

Essential Histories

The Crusades

David Nicolle

For information write to:

FITZROY DEARBORN PUBLISHERS
919 N. Michigan Avenue
Chicago, IL 60611
USA

or

FITZROY DEARBORN PUBLISHERS
310 Regent Street
London W1B 3AX
United Kingdom

Every attempt has been made by the publisher to secure the
appropriate permissions for material reproduced in this book.
If there has been any oversight we will be happy to rectify
the situation and written submissions should be made to the
Publishers.

ISBN 1 57958 354 7

British Library Cataloguing-in-Publication data is available
Library of Congress Cataloging-in-Publication data is available

First published in 2001
Printed and bound in China by L. Rex Printing Company Ltd
01 02 03 04 05   10 9 8 7 6 5 4 3 2 1

For more information about Fitzroy Dearborn Publishers see:
www.fitzroydearborn.com

Contents

Introduction

The Crusades were among the most controversial events during a long rivalry between Christianity and Islam. From Pope Urban II's preaching of what became the First Crusade in 1095 to the fall of Acre in 1291, and the loss of the offshore island of Arwad 11 years later, they formed part of a broader offensive by Western Christendom. This offensive began in the Iberian peninsula much earlier, since when Sicily had also fallen to Norman adventurers from southern Italy while Italian mariners were winning naval superiority throughout most of the Mediterranean.

Before the First Crusade, competition in the Middle East had largely been between the Byzantine or Late Roman Empire and its Islamic neighbours, but this had not involved continuous warfare. Peaceful relations had been the norm, though interrupted by many conflicts. It was the sudden arrival of more fanatical Western Christians – the Crusaders or 'Franks' as they were known in the Middle East – that resulted in two centuries of military struggle.

Even today the Crusades and the *Jihad* 'counter-Crusade' which they stimulated are still seen in a different way by most Western Christians, Orthodox Christians and Muslims. The historical reality of the Crusades was also more complex than the simplistic views that are still used by political, religious and cultural leaders in both East and West. As a result the Crusades and Jihad remained sources of misunderstanding and friction for more than 700 years.

During the 12th and 13th centuries the Crusades were of greater historical importance for Christian Western Europe than for the Islamic world. This was a period of growing confidence in Catholic or 'Latin' Western Europe as well as physical expansion against Muslim, Orthodox Christian and pagan neighbours. Astonishing economic growth was accompanied by a major increase in population while the 12th-century Renaissance produced a burgeoning of art, architecture, literature and learning. During the period of the Crusades Western Europe also learned a great deal from and about its Islamic neighbours. New technology, crops, patterns of trade, trade-goods and philosophical, medical, scientific and geographical knowledge all poured into a Western Europe eager to learn, exploit, dominate and conquer.

The significance of the Crusades for the Orthodox Christian Byzantine Empire, and for Christian communities within the Islamic Middle East, was almost entirely negative. Byzantium was economically and militarily weakened by Western European pressure as well as by the Muslim Turks. Some Christian communities in Syria, Egypt and elsewhere still formed the majority of the population under Islamic rule in the 11th century, but declined into harassed minorities by the 14th century.

Within the Islamic world the Crusades were of only local significance in Syria, Egypt, Anatolia (modern Turkey) and to a lesser extent Iraq. Elsewhere the Crusader conquest of coastal Syria and Palestine was discomforting, but of little immediate concern to rulers and ordinary people. Certainly the Crusades were never seen as a mortal threat to Islam. Nevertheless they and the Jihad which they prompted undermined the old culture of toleration which had characterised the Middle East from the 7th to the 11th centuries. The savagery, intolerance and sheer ignorance shown by Western Europeans encouraged intolerance and conservatism among their victims, and among the *Sunni* Muslim majority this was

The Anglo-Saxons defeat the Danes, shown in an
Anglo-Norman manuscript of c. 1125-50. Both armies
are equipped, mounted and fight in the Norman manner
as fully armoured knights in close-packed *conrois*
squadrons. (*Life of St. Edmund*, Pierpont Morgan Library,
Ms. 736, f.7v, New York)

directed not only against Western European
'barbarians' but also local Christians, Jews
and the *Shi'a* Muslim minority.

Meanwhile the Islamic Middle East
had little to learn from the Western
European 'Franks', who remained inferior in
almost all aspects of culture until the later
13th and 14th centuries. By that time the
Islamic world was rapidly retreating into a
cultural conservatism which made it
virtually impossible for Muslims to accept
lessons from the West. Two centuries of

warfare had, however, created militarily powerful states, the greatest of which was the *Mamluk* Sultanate in Egypt and Syria. These Mamluks halted the Mongol hordes, who had been a genuine threat to Islam, thus enabling Middle Eastern Islamic civilisation to survive and then absorb its invaders. Meanwhile the Mamluks also turned aside to mop up the remnants of the Crusader States.

The so-called Mihrab of the Prophet Sulayman (King Solomon in Judeo-Christian terms) is in the Well of Souls, beneath the famous rock in the Dome of the Rock, Jerusalem. As a *mihrab* it marks the direction of prayer for Muslims, many of whom believe that the souls of all the dead will assemble in this little cave on Judgement Day. The mihrab itself is not only one of the oldest in existence, perhaps dating from at least three centuries before the arrival of the First Crusade, but is virtually unique in having a small piece of meteoric rock embedded in its centre, comparable to the larger meteoric rock which is embedded in one corner of the Kaaba in Mecca. (David Nicolle photograph)

The Mediterranean Sea

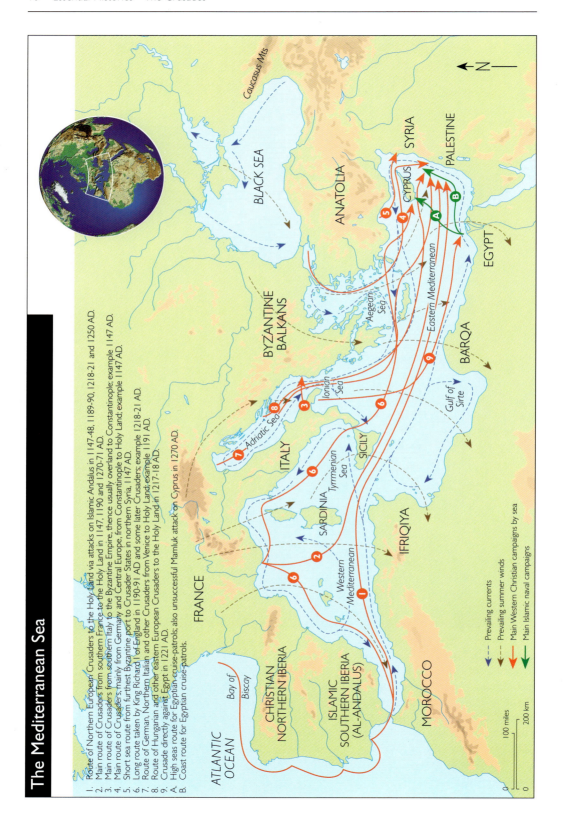

1. Route of Northern European Crusaders to the Holy Land via attacks on Islamic Andalus in 1147-48, 1189-90, 1218-21 and 1250 AD.
2. Main route of Crusaders from southern France to the Holy Land in 1147, 1190 and 1270-71 AD.
3. Main route of Crusaders from southern Italy to the Byzantine Empire, thence usually overland to Constantinople; example 1147 AD.
4. Main route of Crusaders; mainly from Germany and Central Europe, from Constantinople to Holy Land; example 1147 AD.
5. Short sea route from furthest Byzantine port to Crusader States in northern Syria, 1147 AD.
6. Long route taken by King Richard I of England in 1190-91 AD and some later Crusaders; example 1218-21 AD.
7. Route of German, Northern Italian and other Crusaders from Venice to Holy Land; example 1191 AD.
8. Route of Hungarian and other eastern European Crusaders to the Holy Land in 1217-18 AD.
9. Crusade directly against Egypt in 1221 AD.
A. High seas route for Egyptian cruise-patrols; also unsuccessful Mamluk attack on Cyprus in 1270 AD.
B. Coast route for Egyptian cruise-patrols.

Chronology

1071 Byzantine army defeated by Seljuk Turks at Manzikirt.

1081 Alexius I Comnenus becomes Emperor of Byzantium.

1092 Death of Seljuk ruler Malik Shah; fragmentation of the Great Seljuk Empire.

1095 Emperor Alexius I appeals to Western Europe for military support; Pope Urban II preaches what becomes the First Crusade.

1096–99 First Crusade marches east, conquers Jerusalem and starts to carve out four Crusader States.

1101 Crusader army defeated by Turks in Anatolia.

1115 Crusaders defeat Saljuq attempt to retake northern Syria.

1128 Imad al-Din Zangi of Mosul takes Aleppo.

1144 Edessa falls to Zangi.

1146 Zangi succeeded by his son Nur al-Din.

1148 Second Crusade defeated outside Damascus.

1153 Fall of Ascalon to Crusaders.

1154 Nur al-Din takes Damascus.

1163–69 Five attempts by Kingdom of Jerusalem to take control of Egypt.

1169 Saladin takes control of Egypt for Nur al-Din.

1174 Death of Nur al-Din; Saladin takes Damascus.

1176 Byzantine army defeated by Seljuk Turks at Myriokephalon.

1183 Reynald of Châtillon's attempt to attack Mecca defeated; Saladin recognised as overlord of Aleppo.

1187 Saladin defeats Kingdom of Jerusalem at Hattin, reconquers most of the Crusader States.

1189–92 Third Crusade retakes Acre but fails to retake Jerusalem.

1193 Death of Saladin.

1197–98 German Crusade achieves little.

1202–04 Fourth Crusade diverted to conquer Byzantine Constantinople; Crusader States in Greece established.

1218–21 Fifth Crusade invades Egypt; defeated.

1220–22 Mongol invasions of eastern Islamic lands.

1229 Jerusalem returned to Kingdom of Jerusalem by treaty.

1229–42 Civil war in Crusader Kingdom of Cyprus.

1231 Mongol invasion of Iran and Armenia.

1243 Mongols defeat Seljuks of Rum (Anatolia).

1244 Alliance of Crusader States and Syrian Ayyubids defeated at La Forbie by alliance of Khwarazmian refugees from Iran and Ayyubids of Egypt.

1250 Crusade of King Louis IX of France invades Egypt, is defeated; Ayyubid Sultan of Egypt overthrown by Mamluks.

1255–58 Mongols invade Iran and Iraq; civil war in Kingdom of Jerusalem.

1260 Mongols defeated by Mamluks at 'Ayn Jalut.

1261 Byzantines retake Constantinople from 'Latin' Empire.

1263–68 Mamluks reconquer much remaining Crusader territory.

1271–72 Crusade of Prince Edward of England to Palestine.

1275–77 Mamluks ravage Kingdom of Cilician Armenia, defeat Seljuks and Mongols.

1277 Crown of Jerusalem sold to Charles of Anjou, ruler of southern Italy.

1281 Mamluks defeat Mongols and Armenians at Hims.

1289 Mamluks take Tripoli.

1291 Fall of Acre and other Crusader enclaves to Mamluks.

1302 Mamluks take island of Ruad; probable end of Crusader rule at Jubail.

Christendom and Islam in the 11th century

The Crusades were an unusual series of conflicts because they involved three or more distinct groups of people: the Western European Christians, generally known as 'Latins' or 'Franks'; the Muslims of the Middle East and North Africa; the Byzantine and other Orthodox Christians of what are now Turkey and the Balkans, generally known as 'Greeks' to Western Europeans and as 'Rumi' or 'Romans' to their Muslim neighbours. More or less associated with the Orthodox Christian 'Greeks' were many other Christian peoples of the region, most of whom were, in the eyes of Latin-Catholic Christians, schismatics or heretics. Some, such as the Armenians, Georgians and Nubians, had their own independent states. Others, such as the Jacobites and Maronites of Syria, the Copts of Egypt and the Nestorians of Iraq and Iran, formed substantial communities within Islamic states.

The Muslims were similarly divided along linguistic (mainly Arab, Turkish, Kurdish or Persian) and religious lines (Sunni or various Shi'a sects). Other minorities included the Jews, *Druze*, *Yazidis*, *Zoroastrians*, *Manichaean-Paulicians* and others. In the 13th century the Mongols erupted into the Middle East. Included in their ranks were Buddhists, shamanist 'pagans', adherents of various Chinese faiths, Nestorian Christians and even some Muslims.

Some of these peoples had very little contact with each other before the Crusades, while others had co-existed for centuries. The Byzantine Empire and its Islamic neighbours could be called the resident civilisations of the Middle East, and had a long history of both rivalry and peaceful relations. From the 7th to the 10th centuries Islam had been dominant, though its attempts to conquer the Byzantine Empire ended at an early date. Instead these two power blocs reached a

relatively stable relationship with intermittent, small-scale conflict on land and sea. During the late 10th and 11th centuries, as the '*Abbasid Caliphate* of Baghdad fragmented, power shifted back to the Byzantines, who launched a series of major counter-offensives. Then the Byzantine Empire called a halt, drastically reducing its armed forces after having destroyed the Armenian military system that had served as a buffer between Byzantium and the Islamic world for centuries.

For the ordinary people of these regions, an intermittent struggle between the Empire and the Caliphate meant merely a change of masters, and even the military elites often came to terms with their new rulers. In fact this centuries-old rivalry had become political and economic rather than a death-struggle between incompatible cultures.

Guibert of Nogent's explanation of how the Middle East became Muslim; in his history of the First Crusade, written around 1100:

"It is the common opinion, if I understand it correctly, that there was a certain man called Mathomus who drew [those people] away from the belief in the Son and the Holy Spirit and taught them that in the Godhead there was the Father, the Creator, alone. He taught that Jesus Christ was a man without sin. Let me briefly conclude this account of his teaching by saying that he recommended circumcision while completely freeing them [his followers] from restraining their lusts ... [they] do not believe that he [Mathomus] is God, as some people claim, but was a good man and a benefactor through whom they received the Divine Laws."

The coming of the *Seljuk* Turks changed this situation although those Seljuks who overran most of Anatolia (*Rum* or present-day Turkey) remained something of a sideshow as far as the rest of the Islamic world was concerned. Of course the Byzantine perspective was very different. It was the loss of Anatolia to these Turks which prompted Emperor Alexius I to request military help from the West – help which arrived in the unexpected form of a massive Crusade to the Holy Land rather than as pliant mercenaries willing to accept Byzantine authority.

Nevertheless, the impact of the Seljuk Turks upon the Islamic Middle East would

A description of the citizen militia of Syria in the 1080s, by the chronicler Ibn Abu Tayyi', who was writing about his father's lifetime:

"There was no person in Aleppo who did not have military attire in his house, and when war came he would go out at once, fully armed."

prove to be very important. They not only re-established centralised authority, which was inherited by small but still potent successor states, but encouraged a Sunni cultural and religious revival. These Seljuk Turks had not, however, taken full control of the Middle East when the First Crusade arrived. In Egypt and parts of the Palestinian-Syrian coast the Shi'a *Fatimid* Caliphate of Cairo remained a rich and culturally brilliant state. Its relations with the Byzantine Empire and those Italian merchants who were as yet the only Westerners present in the Eastern Mediterranean in any numbers were generally good. Certainly the economic links

Stucco roundel of a seated Islamic ruler with his attendants and guards, 11th century. This form of iconography, with a ruler seated cross-legged on his throne surrounded by members of his court, was traditional in the Islamic world but was rapidly adopted by the Turkish Seljuks, who took control of virtually the entire Middle East in the 11th century. Such stucco roundels were used as architectural decoration in many palaces though this example comes from Rey in Iran. (Museum of Islamic Art and Archaeology, Tehran, Iran. David Nicolle photograph)

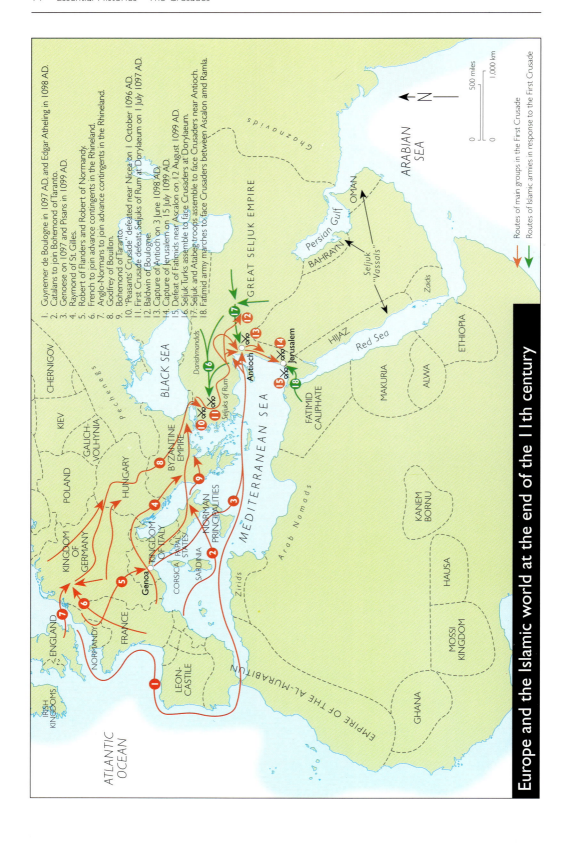

1.   Guynemer de Boulogne in 1097 AD, and Edgar Atheling in 1098 AD.
2.   Catalans to join Bohemond of Taranto.
3.   Genoese on 1097 and Pisans in 1099 AD.
4.   Raymond of St. Gilles.
5.   Robert of Flanders and Robert of Normandy.
6.   French to join advance contingents in the Rhineland.
7.   Anglo-Normans to join advance contingents in the Rhineland.
8.   Godfrey of Bouillon.
9.   Bohemond of Taranto.
10. "Peasants' Crusade" defeated near Nicea on 1 October 1096 AD.
11. First Crusade defeats Seljuks of Rum at Dorylaeum on 1 July 1097 AD.
12. Baldwin of Boulogne.
13. Capture of Antioch on 3 June 1098 AD.
14. Capture of Jerusalem on 15 July 1099 AD.
15. Defeat of Fatimids near Ascalon on 12 August 1099 AD.
16. Seljuk Turks assemble to face Crusaders at Dorylaeum.
17. Seljuk and Atabeg troops assemble to face Crusaders near Antioch.
18. Fatimid army marches to face Crusaders between Ascalon and Ramla.

Routes of main groups in the First Crusade

Routes of Islamic armies in response to the First Crusade

Europe and the Islamic world at the end of the 11th century

between Fatimid Egypt and Italy were already significant.

The relationship between the Byzantine Empire and its Western, Latin-Catholic, fellow Christian neighbours was complex and sometimes unfriendly. The Great Schism (the separation between the Eastern and Western Churches) started in 1054 and was becoming increasingly serious. At first it had meant nothing to ordinary men and women and little to the ruling elites but as the Schism deepened, so people's perceptions of each other grew more hostile. By the 13th century many people in Western Europe maintained that 'Greeks' were worse than 'Saracens'. A century or so later there were those in the Byzantine Empire who preferred domination by Muslim Turks to domination by Western Catholics.

In political and military terms the main arena of conflict between Byzantium and its western neighbours lay in southern Italy, much of which formed part of the Byzantine Empire until its conquest by the Normans.

The ruins of the abandoned city of Fustat still sprawl across parts of southern Cairo. Fustat was the main commercial and residential part of the Egyptian capital during the Fatimid period, in the 11th and 12th centuries. Though devastated by fire during one of the civil wars that characterised the late Fatimid period, part of it was clearly recolonised after Saladin brought stability back to Egypt. The building shown here might have been a mill, perhaps using water which drained into what is now a reed-covered marsh. (David Nicolle photograph)

Subsequently competition moved to the western Balkans where the Norman, then French and finally Spanish rulers of southern Italy sought to extend their authority. In economic terms the Byzantine Empire was also declining in the face of Italian economic, commercial and maritime expansion. Italian merchant republics such as Venice and Genoa certainly took full advantage of Byzantium's weakness.

Before the First Crusade, most Western European states had at best a distant relationship with the Muslims of the Eastern Mediterranean, the only exceptions being

Carving of sleeping guards at the Holy Sepulchre, on a central French capital, early 12th century. This figure is of special interest because the *aventail* of his crudely carved mail *coif* is unlaced, making it fall into a loose triangular shape on his chest. (*in situ* church, Mozac, France. David Nicolle photograph)

some Italian merchant republics plus the Norman kingdom of southern Italy and Sicily. For the merchants of both sides such links were purely commercial. For the Norman elite of southern Italy, however, a different relationship arose after they conquered Sicily. Here a large, highly cultured and militarily important Arab-Islamic minority remained to serve their new Norman Christian rulers. It seems to have maintained cultural links with both Islamic North Africa and with Fatimid Egypt, links which would influence the Siculo-Normans' relations with the Islamic world.

Another important form of contact between Western European society and that of the Islamic Middle East resulted from Christian pilgrimages to Jerusalem and the

Holy Land. The proportion of Westerners who actually made such a pilgrimage was tiny, but their experiences and the significance of travel to the Holy Land gave them considerable influence. Given the confused notions of geography and distance held by most people in Western Europe, the other point of direct contact between Western Christian and Islamic civilisations – namely the Iberian peninsula – must not be ignored. Here Christians and Muslims had been competing for domination for centuries. Although the military struggle remained largely political, a religious or 'crusading' element was increasingly important in what became the Spanish Reconquista. It is also interesting to note that recent Christian victories in Iberia had resulted from a temporary fragmentation of power in the Islamic region known as Andalus (Andalusia). Such successes strengthened the confidence of the Western military elite, particularly in France since French knights had played an important role in the Iberian struggle. Similarly Norman-French and other knights had recently conquered Byzantine southern Italy and seized Sicily from the Muslims.

Whether or not such Western European and above all French military, economic and even cultural confidence made the Crusades inevitable is an unanswerable question. After all, the First Crusade was prompted by a

special set of circumstances in a Byzantine Empire that was under pressure from the Seljuk Turks. Nevertheless, Byzantium's call for help did result in a widespread and virtually uncontrolled mobilisation of Western military might. In such circumstances Western confidence, recent military successes, overpopulation among the military elite and a wave of religious enthusiasm if not outright hysteria probably played their part. Although there was widespread ignorance of the realities of the task to be attempted, there was surely an element of economic opportunism on the part of some better informed Italian participants.

Such factors might explain the fact that the First Crusade or 'armed pilgrimage' remained a unique historical phenomenon. Different factors led to the wars of the Crusades continuing for two centuries, or more if the so-called 'Later Crusades' are included. For a start the First Crusade was an astonishing success. No subsequent expedition succeeded to anything like the same degree, and all, except for the Fourth Crusade which was diverted against Byzantium, were more or less failures. Indeed it took a century for Western political, military, religious and cultural leaderships to accept the fact that the First Crusade was a 'one off'. Enthusiasm for the concept of Crusade steadily declined, first among ordinary people, then among the military aristocracy and cultural elite. Finally even the Church recognised this reality.

On the other side of the religious frontier, enthusiasm for Jihad or counter-Crusade increased, and after the Mamluks finally expelled the descendants of the Crusaders from Palestine and Syria in the late 13th century the torch of Jihad was passed to the Ottoman Turks. Their subsequent wave of conquest took them into southern Russia, to the gates of Vienna, to Arabia, North Africa and even further afield. In fact it could be claimed that by preaching the First Crusade, Pope Urban II sowed the wind, and that his successors reaped the whirlwind.

Nizam al-Mulk, a wazir *or chief minister of the Seljuk sultan Malik-Shah, described in his* Siyasat Nama *treatise on government written in 1091 the ideal training programme for* ghulam *or mamluk soldiers after they had been purchased as slaves:*

"One year on foot at the stirrup of a rider, wearing a [plain] Zandaniji cloak ... Next given a small Turkish horse, a saddle covered in untanned leather, a plain bridle and stirrup leathers. In this manner to serve one year with a horse and whip. In the third year they are given a belt. In the fourth year they are given a quiver and bowcase which is attached to the belt when they are mounted. In the fifth year they are given a better saddle and a decorated bridle, plus a handsome cloak and a mace which he hangs in a mace-ring."

Subsequent promotions concern duties rather than appearance or equipment, except in the eighth year, when they were given a black felt hat decorated with silver wire, and a fine cloak from Ganja.

Byzantines, Turks, Crusaders and Saracens

Crusader armies

Most of those involved in the First Crusade were relatively prosperous and the idea that Crusading was a means of escape for poor knights seeking their fortune overseas is largely a myth. The bulk of the cavalry were knights (or were from that minor military elite which would become knights in the 12th century), while the infantry appears to have been largely drawn from professional soldiers, prosperous peasants or townsmen. Meanwhile the role of women was largely as financial backers rather than active participants.

Military recruitment within the Crusader States, once these had been established, differed considerably from that of Crusading expeditions. The majority of the nobility were also from modest knightly families rather than the great aristocracy of Western Europe. The number of knights available to the Crusader States was correspondingly small, while a lack of agricultural land meant that the bulk of the military aristocracy were urban based like those of northern Italy. Non-knightly troops included professional infantry and cavalry *sergeants* paid by towns or the Church. In an emergency a general feudal levy or *arrière ban* added local Arabic-speaking Christians and Armenians to the existing urban militias. Nevertheless, professional mercenaries remained an essential element and governments generally preferred a steady supply of such men to the temporary appearance of over-enthusiastic Crusaders.

The Crusader States would not accept defeated Muslim troops into their service unless they converted to Christianity. Such converts played a significant role as *turcopoles*, mostly serving as light cavalry and some horse-archers. As the power of the Crusader States declined, so the importance

Statuette of knight, French 11th–12th centuries. A large number of such statuettes, often designed for use as wine or water-pouring containers, survive from the 13th and 14th centuries. This, however, is one of the few which dates from the 12th century or even earlier. Bronze statuettes, being three-dimensional, provide better details of the way in which sword-belts were worn and shields carried by the early Crusader military elite. (inv. O.A. 9103, Musée du Louvre, Paris, France)

Part of a letter from Pope Celestine III written in 1195, urging Christians to go on Crusade, as included in the chronicle of Ralph of Diceto:

"We should not be amazed at those, including several of the world's princes, who have so far set out to fight the Saracen heathen with spear and sword, even though they have accomplished nothing wholly successful ... Let those who have carried military arms among Christian folk now take up the Sign of the Cross and let them neither despair for their small numbers nor glory in their multitude."

of the Military Orders grew. Initially their recruits needed only to be free men, but later those becoming 'brother knights' were of knightly origin while 'brother sergeants' were mostly of free peasant or artisan families.

Most early Crusading expeditions were organised around the most senior barons taking part, though ordinary infantry often fought in groupings that reflected their country of origin. By the 13th century Crusading expeditions were more structured, even to the extent that knights of differing status were expected to have different numbers of horses and followers. Meanwhile the military organisation of the Crusader States was essentially the same as that in Western Europe. The command structure of such armies remained essentially amateur, though the king, as overall commander, clearly consulted his leading barons and the Masters of the Military Orders. As the secular armies of the Crusader States declined, those of the Military Orders increased in effectiveness, with each Order providing what was effectively a regiment of professional soldiers.

By the 13th century major offensive operations had to await the arrival of a Crusade from the West. These never lost a broader strategic vision, with the conquest of Egypt being a common objective. Nevertheless, most Crusades were reactive rather than proactive. The precise function of Crusader castles remains a matter of

Battle scene on a painted paper fragment, Egypt 12th century. This well-known picture was found in the ruins of Fustat and clearly shows a battle outside a fortified city or castle between the Muslim garrison and a force of Western Europeans including knights. The latter are probably Crusaders and the fortification might represent Ascalon, which the Fatimid Egyptians held against constant Crusader attack for several decades. The Muslims include a fully armoured horseman in a mail hauberk, but with a bulky turban rather than a helmet. The archers on the walls are similarly protected whereas two Muslim foot soldiers are protected only by their larger shields. The presumed Crusaders include a knight in typical and accurately illustrated 12th-century armour, mail hauberk, shield, and riding an unarmoured horse. Only part of the attacking foot soldier in the top right corner survives, and he is more problematical, being equipped with a round shield, a sword and a helmet. (Department of Oriental Antiquities, British Museum, London, England)

debate. They could not really 'plug' an invasion route and their usefulness as refuges was limited. However, even in the defensive environment of the 13th century such secure bases enabled garrisons to raid enemy territory and harass invaders.

Remarkably little is known about the training of Western European armies at the time of the Crusades. For cavalry the primary emphasis was on the lance as used in close-packed conrois formations. Another very important aspect of Western European military training concerned the crossbow, which was the most effective weapon available to European infantry.

Byzantine armies

The Byzantine Empire's loss of much of Anatolia deprived it of its most important source of military manpower, and at the end of the 11th century foreign troops probably outnumbered domestic recruits. Attempts to rebuild a 'national' army were only partially successful and foreign mercenaries continued to play a major role. The long-established Byzantine practice of enlisting prisoners-of-war also continued. By the late 12th and 13th centuries a provincial elite known as *archontes* emerged, having clear military

authority though no apparent legal status. After the Fourth Crusade conquered Constantinople (Istanbul) and large parts of the Empire's Greek heartland, the fragmented Byzantine successor states had much reduced sources of recruitment. Nevertheless, the 'Empire' of Nicea (Iznik) continued to enlist Western mercenaries.

Byzantine armies of the 12th and 13th centuries inherited one of the most ancient military organisations in the medieval world, but they were rarely in a position to take full advantage of it. The armed forces basically consisted of two armies – one in the western

Al-Tarsusi, in the section of his military training manual dealing with archery (late 12th century drawing on an 8th–9th century original):

"When shooting at a horseman who is not moving, aim at his saddle-bow so that you will hit the man if the arrow goes high, or the horse if it goes low. If his back is turned, aim at the spot between his shoulders. If he is charging with a sword, shoot at him but not from too far away, for if you miss him he might strike you with his sword [before you can shoot again]."

Above and opposite: Warriors on carved ivory box, Byzantine 11th–12th centuries. Most Byzantine representations of warriors, particularly those in a religious context, give the men archaic pseudo-Roman equipment that probably did not reflect current reality. On this ivory box, however, three panels seem to be more realistic and only the naked man can be dismissed as an ancient artistic convention. The kneeling warrior with a helmet, bow, spear, shield and sword with a curved sabre-style hilt seems especially contemporary. (Hermitage Museum, St Petersburg, Russia. David Nicolle photographs)

or European provinces and one in the eastern or Asian provinces — plus a small fleet. In reality the Byzantines never recovered from the disasters of the later 11th century. The army also adopted organisational structures, equipment and tactics from its Western European rivals and its Turkish neighbours. After western Anatolia was regained in the early 12th century the territory was secured by a broad strip of depopulated no-man's-land dotted with powerful fortresses and supported by field armies from the centre of the Empire.

More is known about training in the period before the Crusades than during the 12th and 13th centuries. By the 11th century horse-archery had been added to traditional skills with other weapons. Infantry archers were still theoretically trained to shoot in

disciplined ranks by command. During the 12th century the apparent success of Western European Crusading armies also led to an emphasis on Western military skills.

Islamic armies

The armies of the Islamic Middle East were remarkably varied. Recruitment reflected whatever suitable manpower was available, plus as many Central Asian Turkish mamluk or ghulam slave-origin professional soldiers as could be afforded. The rest of a *jund* army usually consisted of local Turks, Kurds, Arabs, Persians, Armenians and others. Many cities had their own militia, sometimes called an *ahdath*. Numerous religiously motivated volunteers or *mutatawi'ah* also took part in campaigns against the Crusaders.

The armed forces of Fatimid Egypt were different. They were based upon a classical model provided by the 9th-century 'Abbasid Caliphate. Infantry regiments consisted of black African slave-soldiers, many Christian Armenians and some Iranians. The cavalry included Syrian Arabs, Turkish ghulams, Europeans of slave and perhaps mercenary origin, Armenians and perhaps Iranians. The Fatimids also had a substantial navy. These military systems were inherited by Saladin.

His army was largely Turkish, with its *halqa* elite consisting of mamluks. The army of the subsequent Mamluk Sultanate was essentially the same as those of the preceding *Ayyubid* states, though Turkish mamluks now formed the ruling as well as military elite. The Seljuks of Rum or Anatolia tried to model their army on that of their great Seljuk predecessors. Slave-origin ghulams formed a core around which tribal Turks, assimilated Greeks, Armenian and others, plus a remarkable assortment of mercenaries assembled.

The success of Islamic armies in containing and then expelling the Crusaders reflected their superior organisation, logistical support, discipline and tactics. They, like the Byzantines, were heirs to a sophisticated military tradition where the 'men of the sword' or soldiers were supported by the 'men of the pen' or civilian administrators, government officials and bureaucrats. Large armies such as that of the Ayyubids were divided into units, often with specific functions, but equally important were the *atlab al-mira*

supply train and the *suq al-'askar* mobile 'army market'.

Strategy and even tactics in the Islamic Middle East were greatly influenced by ecological factors such as summer heat, winter rain, the availability of water and pasture and the need to harvest crops. The Islamic states also learned that the only way to overcome the Crusader States was by the steady reduction of their fortified towns and castles. Training in larger armies seems to have relied on written textbooks to a greater extent than anywhere else, except perhaps China. For cavalry this involved individual skill with numerous weapons plus a variety of unit manoeuvres. Infantry were expected to practise archery, avoid and harass enemy cavalry, and know the skills of siege warfare.

A less well-known fragment of a Fatimid drawing on paper, again from Fustat, shows the head of an infantryman armed with two javelins. His head is protected by a bulky turban with the ends of its cloth pulled up into a sort of point. He also carries a round or perhaps kite-shaped shield. Egypt 11th-12th centuries. (Ms. inv. 13801, Museum of Islamic Art, Cairo, Egypt. David Nicolle photograph)

The First Crusade

In 1071 the Byzantine army was catastrophically defeated by the Seljuk Turks at the battle of Manzikirt, after which the Byzantine Empire endured political chaos, civil war and the loss of virtually the whole of Anatolia. This was the real background to the First Crusade. In 1081, a general named Alexius Comnenus seized the throne and reimposed government control across what was left of the Byzantine Empire, despite attacks by the Seljuk Turks, the pagan Pecheneg Turks and the Normans of southern Italy. In 1095 Alexius sent a message to Pope Urban II asking for Western mercenary troops.

Quite why this simple request resulted in a massive Crusade remains unclear, but the basic facts are known. Pope Urban II preached a sort of armed pilgrimage which would help the Byzantines and also retake the Holy Land. This idea caught on and in November 1095 Pope Urban called upon the military elite of Western Christendom to 'liberate' Jerusalem from the 'infidels'. The subsequent wave of enthusiasm was most notable among the lower levels of a military elite that was evolving into what became the knightly class. Many ordinary people were also caught up in the religious hysteria, though the ruling class tended to be less enthusiastic.

The moment seemed appropriate. Emperor Alexius was well aware of conditions within the neighbouring Islamic states while the Papacy in Rome probably had comparable information. The idea that the First Crusade marched eastward with little knowledge of their destination is probably a myth, at least as far as those who were directing the movement. Within the Middle East the once mighty Seljuk Sultanate, which had permitted a small army to attack the Byzantines back in the 1070s, was now fragmenting. Seljuk and other Turkish *amirates* in Anatolia and Armenia were effectively independent, as were the *atabeg* statelets of Syria and northern Iraq. Most still acknowledged the suzereinty of the Great Seljuk Sultan but in reality the First Crusade, supported by the Byzantines, faced a chronically divided Islamic world. This fragmentation was most acute in Syria and Palestine, the Crusaders' destination. Meanwhile the Fatimid Caliphate in Egypt was enjoying a modest revival. It had never accepted the loss of Palestine and western Syria to the Seljuk Turks and would take advantage of the approaching Crusade to regain Jerusalem.

All these Islamic states, Sunni and Shi'a, were, however, preoccupied with their own rivalries. Confident of their military superiority over the Byzantines, and secure in their superior wealth, science, technology, material culture, great cities and far-ranging trade networks, the Islamic peoples never seem to have expected that a horde of heavily armed religious fanatics would descend upon them from Western Europe. For the Islamic Middle East, if not for Andalus and North Africa, Western Europe was a cultural and military backwater.

Such a judgement was seriously out of date. The *Ifranj* or 'Franks' may still have been relatively primitive compared to Byzantines or Muslims, but they were no longer the unwashed barbarians of a century or so earlier. In military terms Italy, Spain and much of France and England were on a similar level to the Byzantine Empire. Indeed, France would become the powerhouse of the Crusading movement. For their part the Armenians, previously crushed between Byzantines and Muslims, were now taking control of large areas of south-central Anatolia, to become a major military presence when the First Crusade burst upon the scene.

Pope Urban II and the Emperor Alexius I were prime movers but neither actually led the Crusade. Similarly the commanders of the First Crusade often found themselves responding to what the mass of participants demanded. In fact military leadership of this extraordinary expedition was collective, with each regional or linguistic contingent following the senior lord within its ranks. During the course of the campaign some showed greater capabilities than others, such as Bohemond of Taranto, and they were temporarily recognised as senior – but only while a crisis existed. Others, such as

Raymond of St Gilles and Robert of Normandy, tried to assume superiority through their status, wealth or the size of their military contingent. The result was a division of command at crucial moments. Indeed the success of the First Crusade, despite such drawbacks, seemed virtually miraculous, 'Favoured by God' in the eyes of most Christians. Godfrey of Bouillon, who became titular leader with the re-establishment of Christian rule in Jerusalem, reflected the paradox of leadership in this 'Divinely inspired' movement, refusing to wear a king's crown in the city where Christ wore a crown of thorns.

There was a similar lack of cohesive leadership on the Islamic side. In Iran the Great Seljuk Sultan Berk Yaruq was preoccupied with the fragmentation of his own realm. Resistance was left to local rulers and governors. Many fought hard but were individually overwhelmed by the armoured horde from the west. Other local leaders came to terms or even tried to form alliances with these fearsome newcomers, and the fact that some Muslim leaders thought the invaders could be used in this way illustrates their lack of understanding of what the First Crusade was all about. Such a lack of mutual support among local Muslim rulers shocked some of their own people, though it would take a long time for their successors to overcome the chronic political, ethnic and religious divisions within Middle Eastern Islam.

As the Crusaders made their way east by land and sea, the first blood to be spilled in large quantities was not Muslim but Jewish. In what has been called 'the first Holocaust' some sections of what was clearly a

Infantryman with tall shield on a lustreware ceramic plate, Iran or Egypt 12th century. The foot soldier on this magnificent ceramic has a straight sword with the kind of hilt which appears in several Islamic manuscripts from this period. The hilt was probably of cast bronze. His tall shield with its flattened base and chequerboard pattern is a *januwiya*, a form of infantry mantlet whose name suggests that it was of Italian origin. Genoa, from which the name derives, became one of the main Italian merchant republics through which military equipment and strategic materials were illegally sold to the Islamic states during the Crusader period. (De Unger Collection, London)

religiously excited horde of armed men and their followers turned upon the Jews of Germany. As the Crusades continued various Crusader contingents reached what was for them alien territory in Catholic Hungary and even more so in the Orthodox Christian Balkans. As a result many local people came to view them as little better than bandits. When the Crusaders reached the Byzantine capital of Constantinople further trouble was avoided by the diplomatic skill of Emperor Alexius, while Crusader leaders from Norman Italy generally maintained tighter control over their troops than did other leaders from France or Germany.

The first major clash between Crusaders and Muslims was a disaster for the Christians. It happened when the so-called Peasants' Crusade, which marched a year ahead of the main Crusade, entered Seljuk Turkish territory in Anatolia. There it was virtually exterminated on 21 October 1096. The first units of the First Crusade proper reached Constantinople two months later, but it was not until early April the following year that the assembled contingents of the First Crusade were ferried across to the Asian shore in Byzantine ships. On 14 May 1097, they and their Byzantine allies attacked the Anatolian Seljuk capital of Nicea. (This surrendered to the Byzantines rather than the bloodthirsty Crusaders on 26 June, much to the annoyance of the latter.) From then on relations between Crusaders and the Byzantine authorities, never very good, gradually deteriorated.

The Crusaders' first full-scale battle took place on 1 July 1097 and, although it was a close run thing, it ended in total victory for the Christians. Hunger, hardship and the seizure of cities, some of which were then garrisoned by Emperor Alexius' troops and some of which were retaken by the Seljuks, marked their subsequent march across Anatolia. The Crusaders' next major military obstacle was the great Syrian city of Antioch (now Antakya in Turkey). Here the Crusaders not only conducted an epic siege but also defeated two largely Turkish armies. One was attempting to relieve the city, the other to retake Antioch, which had fallen to the

invaders just over three weeks previously on
3 June 1098.

Reinforcements also reached the Crusaders
in the form of fleets from Italy, England and
elsewhere. These not only enabled the

The Church of St Peter, a short distance from the city of
Antakya (Antioch), was the most sacred site in the
Crusader Principality of Antioch. The apostle Peter and
the first Christians are believed to have used the cave as
a church. The present simple structure incorporates
elements built across the front of what is largely a man-
made cave in the side of the mountain during the
Crusader occupation in the 12th and 13th centuries.
(David Nicolle photograph)

*Fulcher of Chartres on the appalling
conditions endured by the Crusaders
outside Antioch:*

"We felt that misfortunes had befallen
the Franks because of their sins and for
that reason they were not able to take
the city for so long a time. Luxury and
avarice and pride and plunder had
indeed weakened them. Then the
Franks, having consulted together,
expelled the women from the army, the
married as well as unmarried, lest defiled
by the sordidness of riotous living they
should displease the Lord."

invaders to re-establish contact with Western
Europe and bring supplies as well as men, but
also more than compensated for the presence
of a Fatimid Egyptian fleet in the Eastern
Mediterranean. Not that the Fatimid
government had been idle. Taking advantage
of the Seljuks' difficulties in northern Syria,
its army retook Jerusalem and most of
Palestine while reinforcing the garrisons of
several coastal ports. The Fatimids even tried
to negotiate an anti-Seljuk alliance with the
Crusaders, presumably still mistaking them
for an offshoot of the Byzantine Empire with

which the Fatimid Caliphate had often enjoyed good relations. Of course the Crusaders, so close to their goal of Jerusalem and in a high state of religious enthusiasm, were not interested. The result was the siege and capture of the Holy City, which fell on 15 July 1099, followed by the first of several major battles between Fatimid armies and Crusader forces on the coastal plain near Ascalon. The First Crusade had been crowned with what was even then regarded as an almost miraculous success – a success which would not, however, be repeated.

The so-called Tower of David in Jerusalem stands against the western wall of the Old City. This was the city's Citadel in medieval times and the highest point of the fortifications which were also the most vulnerable. There had been a citadel here since Herodian or Roman times, but this fell into decay during the peaceful early Islamic Arab era. It was rebuilt during the Crusader occupation, thereafter being maintained and perhaps strengthened under the Mamluks and Ottomans. (David Nicolle photograph)

Extract from a letter, found in the Cairo synagogue, written by Yesha'ya ha-Kohen Ben Masliah, concerning Jewish prisoners taken by the First Crusade:

"News still reaches us that amongst those who were redeemed from the Franks and remain in Ascalon some are in danger of dying of want. Others remained in captivity, and yet others were killed before the eyes of the rest … In the end all those who could be ransomed from them were liberated, and only a few whom they kept remained in their hands … To this day these captives remain in their hands, as well as those who were taken at Antioch, but these are few, not counting those who abjured their faith because they lost patience as it was not possible to ransom them and because they despaired of being permitted to go free."

Carving of St George helping the First Crusaders outside Antioch, English early 12th century. The story was popular throughout most of Latin Western Europe during the period of the Crusades, but this is one of the earliest and best preserved carved reliefs. At this date the only item of military equipment which differentiates the Crusaders praying on the left, from the Muslims being slaughtered by St George on the right, is the latters' round shields. The round shield became, in fact, the most common iconographic method of identifying 'infidel' troops in medieval European art.
(*in situ* parish church of St George, Fordington, England. David Nicolle photograph)

Ibn al-Qalanisi describing the defence of Tyre against Crusader attack in 1111–12:
"A long timber beam was set up on the wall in front of the [enemy] siege-tower. On top of it, forming a T-shaped cross, another beam forty cubits long was swung on pulleys worked by a winch in the manner as a ship's mast ... At one end of the pivoting beam was an iron spar and at the other end ropes running through pulleys by means of which the operators could hoist buckets of dung and refuse and empty them over the Franks ... Then this sailor (who had designed the device) had panniers and baskets filled with oil, pitch, wood shavings, resin and cane-bark set on fire and hoisted up in the manner described to the level of the Frankish tower (which was then burned down)."

Crusade and jihad; consolidation of Islamic resistance

The so-called Peasants' Crusade had been wiped out on the frontier of Islamic territory. The second wave, or the First Crusade proper, had achieved an almost miraculous success at Antioch, in defeating two large Islamic armies and by seizing the Holy City of Jerusalem. A third wave was crushed in eastern Anatolia while apparently heading for Iraq. Whether or not this third wave was hoping to take the great city of Baghdad, which Western Christians regarded as the 'capital' of the Islamic world, has never been established. The result was, however, a catastrophe and never again would Crusading armies have a clear passage through Muslim-Turkish Anatolia. Instead the Mediterranean became the main, and eventually the only, link between the Crusader States and Western Europe.

Those of the First Crusade who remained in the east, plus a steady flow of newcomers from Europe, joined forces with the Armenians to carve out four small states in what are now south-eastern Turkey, Syria, Lebanon, Palestine and Jordan. They became the Principality of Antioch, the County of Edessa, the County of Tripoli and the Kingdom of Jerusalem. A fifth state, that of the Armenians themselves, emerged in what is now Turkish Cilicia.

Fully aware that control of the coast was essential for their survival, the Christians soon took all the ports except Ascalon, which remained in Fatimid hands for several decades. In fact Ascalon became a 12th-century version of the 20th- to 21st-century Gaza Strip. Nevertheless, the invaders soon suffered serious reverses, partly through their own overconfidence and partly because their Muslim neighbours recovered from the initial shock of invasion. In 1100 Bohemond of Taranto, Prince of Antioch and perhaps the most skilful military leader in Crusader

ranks, was captured. Later that year Godfrey of Bouillon, ruler of Crusader Jerusalem, died and was succeeded by Baldwin of Boulogne, the Count of Edessa. Meanwhile the Fatimid army, though far past its peak, launched a series of campaign which resulted in the three battles of Ramla. The Egyptians were defeated in the first and third, but in the second battle they virtually exterminated a Crusader army, causing losses which the Christians could not afford.

In the north the fortunes of war were similarly divided and although the Crusaders won notable victories, their glory days were soon over. Nevertheless, it took several decades for the Western Christians to realise that the clear military superiority they had enjoyed during the First Crusade no longer existed. From then on the Crusaders were forced on to the defensive, while the Muslims slowly reunited their forces and,

Bohemond of Taranto
Bohemond, born in the mid-1050s, eldest son of Robert Guiscard, fought alongside his father against Emperor Alexius in the early 1080s. He joined the First Crusade, became its most effective military commander and subsequently the ruler of Antioch. Having taken an oath of allegiance to Emperor Alexius, Bohemond refused to recognise the Byzantine claim to Antioch, hence there were tensions. He was captured by Danishmandid Turks in 1100 but released in 1103. After further clashes with the Byzantines in Cilicia, he returned to Italy from where he unsuccessfully attacked Byzantine Albania in 1107. Bohemond did not return to Syria but died in Apulia in 1111.

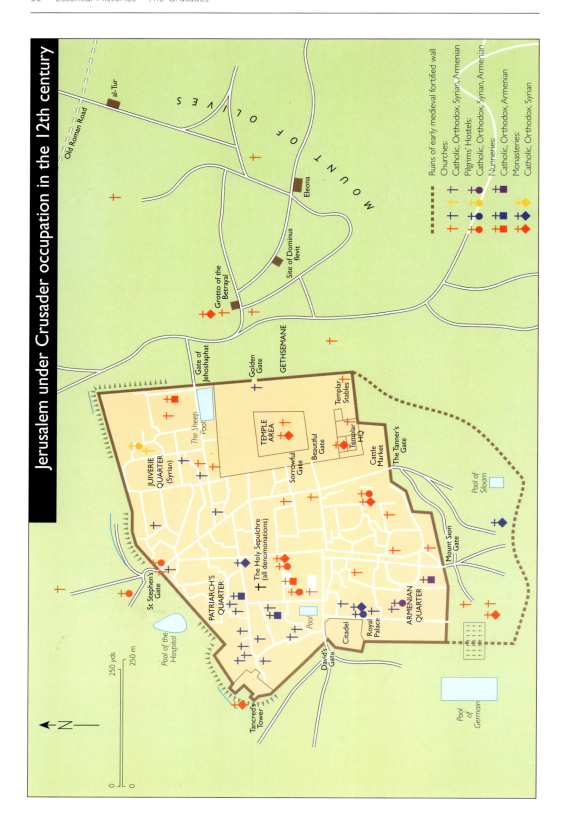

Jerusalem under Crusader occupation in the 12th century

Ruins of early medieval fortified wall

Churches:
Catholic, Orthodox, Syrian, Armenian

Pilgrims' Hostels:
Catholic, Orthodox, Syrian, Armenian

Nunneries:
Catholic, Orthodox, Armenian

Monasteries:
Catholic, Orthodox, Syrian

MOUNT OF OLIVES

Old Roman Road

al-Tur

Eleona

Site of Dominus flevit

Grotto of the Betrayal

GETHSEMANE

Gate of Jehoshaphat

Golden Gate

The Sheep Pool

TEMPLE AREA

Beautiful Gate

Sorrowful Gate

Templar Stables

Templar HQ

Cattle Market

The Tanner's Gate

Pool of Siloam

JUIVERIE QUARTER (Syrian)

The Holy Sepulchre (all denominations)

PATRIARCH'S QUARTER

St Stephen's Gate

Pool of the Hospital

Pool

Citadel

Royal Palace

David's Gate

Tancred's Tower

ARMENIAN QUARTER

Mount Sion Gate

Pool of Germain

250 yds

250 m

N

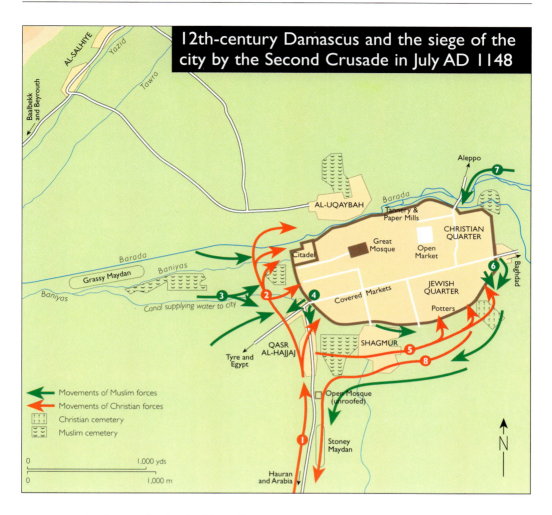

12th-century Damascus and the siege of the city by the Second Crusade in July AD 1148

even more slowly, retook what had been lost in the early 12th century.

In strategic terms the Crusader States were vulnerable, forming an arc of territory from the unclear eastern frontier of the County of Edessa to the southern tip of the Kingdom of Jerusalem. To the north were the similarly newly established Turkish Anatolian states of the Danishmandids and Seljuks. To the east lay the great city of Mosul which would become the power-house of the first Islamic counter-Crusade. Tucked inside the curve of Crusader territory was the seemingly vulnerable Syrian city of Aleppo which the Christians never took. Further south, and as yet of secondary significance, was another great Syrian city – Damascus – which again the Crusaders never took. Beyond Damascus

Fulcher of Chartres on the role of women in the defence of Crusader Jaffa against a Fatimid naval assault in 1123:

"The Arab or Aethiopian [Sudanese] foot soldiers which they brought with them together with a body of cavalry, made a heavy assault upon the inhabitants of Jaffa. On both sides men hurled javelins, some threw stones and others shot arrows. Moreover those within the city, fighting manfully for themselves, slew those outside with oft-repeated blows … The women of Jaffa were constantly ready with generous help for the men who were struggling mightily. Some carried stones and others brought water to drink."

As yet the Crusader States largely ignored the Byzantine Empire's attempts to exert its own suzereinty over them. Instead an uneasy alliance was formed, though the Byzantines continued to try to dominate Antioch. The rulers of Damascus were afraid of being taken over by their fellow-Muslim rulers of Mosul and so formed occasional alliances with the Crusader States. In fact King Baldwin I of Jerusalem and Tughtagin, the amir of Damascus, agreed to share the revenues of territory south of Damascus and east of the Jordan. Meanwhile Edessa, where the Crusader military elite were so few that they relied on Armenian military support, survived because the Muslim rulers of Aleppo felt themselves to be threatened by the other more powerful Crusader States.

This fragile equilibrium collapsed in the mid-12th century as the fragmented Islamic states gradually coalesced into fewer realms. As the shock of the First Crusade wore off,

the Christians took control of almost all the agricultural zone, establishing a hazy frontier with the semi-desert regions. The latter, though sometimes recognising the authority of one or other Islamic ruler, had been independent for centuries, the only exception being the Islamic holy land of the Hijaz in Arabia which recognised a distant Seljuk overlordship. To the west the Sinai desert nominally formed part of Fatimid territory. Finally there was the Fatimid-held port and enclave of Ascalon on the Mediterranean whose survival largely depended upon the Fatimid-Egyptian navy. Only when Italian naval power became overwhelming did the Crusaders finally take Ascalon in 1153. This event also opened the way for Crusader attempts to take control of Egypt, where Fatimid power was tottering to its fall. But Egypt's weakness also attracted attempts by Nur al-Din, the increasingly powerful Turkish ruler of northern Iraq and Syria, to win control of what all sides recognised as a potential power-house. It was Nur al-Din and in particular his governor Salah al-Din (Saladin) who eventually succeeded.

The *maristan* or hospital of Nur al-Din in the Old City of Damascus is one of the best preserved medieval hospitals in the Middle East. Nur al-Din was, of course, a great patron of art, architecture and public works as well as being perhaps the most significant figure in the Islamic military revival of the 12th century. The maristan itself was built to treat those suffering from mental health problems, being designed to provide not only secure accommodation but also a soothing environment in which fountains and a large pool were central features. The doctors themselves worked and taught in the four surrounding *iwans* or tall shaded recesses in each wall. Today the maristan of Nur al-Din is a museum of Arab-Islamic Science and Medicine. (David Nicolle photograph)

Guibert of Nogent on how a doctor proposed treating the injured King Baldwin I of Jerusalem who had a deep wound in his body:

"He proposed a wonderful expedient … He asked the king that he might order one of the Saracen prisoners to be wounded in the same position as the king himself and then order him to be killed so that the doctor might investigate freely on the dead body and examine certainly from looking at it what the royal wound was like on its inside."

The king refused, but had a bear wounded and killed instead.

the Islamic military elite returned to its traditional responsibilities of jihad or the defence and recovery of Islamic territory. In general, Middle Eastern society regarded the presence of Crusader States in the heart of the Islamic world as an affront rather than a threat. For their part the Crusader Kings of Jerusalem seem to have neglected the rising power of Mosul, only recognising the threat from the east when Mosul and Aleppo were united under the rule of Imad al-Din Zangi in 1128 and more particularly when Zangi conquered most of the County of Edessa in 1144. Instead their attention was focused largely upon Damascus and Egypt.

Nevertheless, the fall of Edessa sent shockwaves throughout Western Christendom and resulted in the preaching of the Second Crusade by St Bernard of Clairvaux. In 1147 two great expeditions set out from France and Germany. Unlike the First Crusade, the Second came to grief in

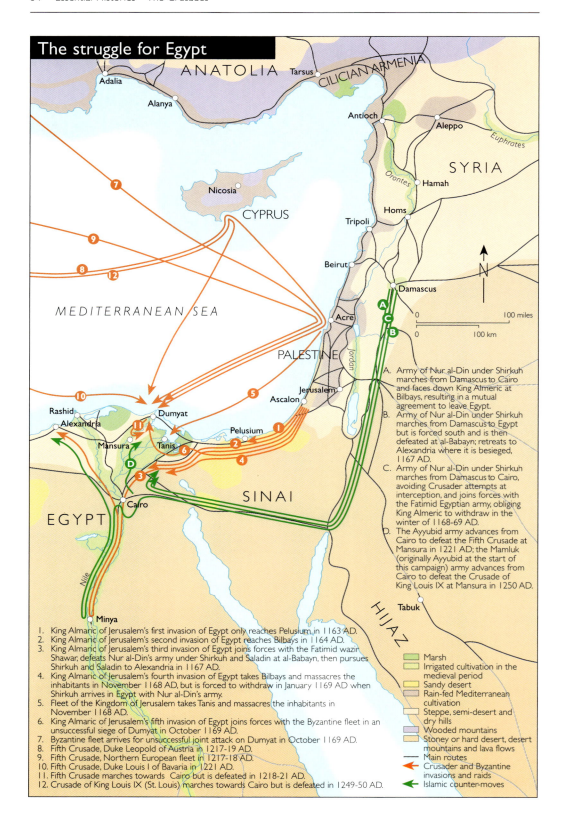

The struggle for Egypt

ANATOLIA   Tarsus   CILICIAN ARMENIA

Adalia

Alanya

Antioch

Aleppo

Euphrates

SYRIA

Nicosia

Orontes   Hamah

CYPRUS

Homs

Tripoli

Beirut

Damascus

MEDITERRANEAN SEA

Acre

PALESTINE

Jordan

Jerusalem

Ascalon

Rashid

Dumyat

Alexandria

Pelusium

Mansura   Tanis

EGYPT   Cairo

SINAI

Nile

HIJAZ

Tabuk

Minya

N

0   100 miles

0   100 km

A. Army of Nur al-Din under Shirkuh marches from Damascus to Cairo and faces down King Almeric at Bilbays, resulting in a mutual agreement to leave Egypt.
B. Army of Nur al-Din under Shirkuh marches from Damascus to Egypt but is forced south and is then defeated at al-Babayn; retreats to Alexandria where it is besieged, 1167 AD.
C. Army of Nur al-Din under Shirkuh marches from Damascus to Cairo, avoiding Crusader attempts at interception, and joins forces with the Fatimid Egyptian army, obliging King Almeric to withdraw in the winter of 1168–69 AD.
D. The Ayyubid army advances from Cairo to defeat the Fifth Crusade at Mansura in 1221 AD; the Mamluk (originally Ayyubid at the start of this campaign) army advances from Cairo to defeat the Crusade of King Louis IX at Mansura in 1250 AD.

1. King Almaric of Jerusalem's first invasion of Egypt only reaches Pelusium in 1163 AD.
2. King Almaric of Jerusalem's second invasion of Egypt reaches Bilbays in 1164 AD.
3. King Almaric of Jerusalem's third invasion of Egypt joins forces with the Fatimid wazir Shawar, defeats Nur al-Din's army under Shirkuh and Saladin at al-Babayn, then pursues Shirkuh and Saladin to Alexandria in 1167 AD.
4. King Almaric of Jerusalem's fourth invasion of Egypt takes Bilbays and massacres the inhabitants in November 1168 AD, but is forced to withdraw in January 1169 AD when Shirkuh arrives in Egypt with Nur al-Din's army.
5. Fleet of the Kingdom of Jerusalem takes Tanis and massacres the inhabitants in November 1168 AD.
6. King Almaric of Jerusalem's fifth invasion of Egypt joins forces with the Byzantine fleet in an unsuccessful siege of Dumyat in October 1169 AD.
7. Byzantine fleet arrives for unsuccessful joint attack on Dumyat in October 1169 AD.
8. Fifth Crusade, Duke Leopold of Austria in 1217–19 AD.
9. Fifth Crusade, Northern European fleet in 1217–18 AD.
10. Fifth Crusade, Duke Louis I of Bavaria in 1221 AD.
11. Fifth Crusade marches towards Cairo but is defeated in 1218–21 AD.
12. Crusade of King Louis IX (St. Louis) marches towards Cairo but is defeated in 1249–50 AD.

- Marsh
- Irrigated cultivation in the medieval period
- Sandy desert
- Rain-fed Mediterranean cultivation
- Steppe, semi-desert and dry hills
- Wooded mountains
- Stoney or hard desert, desert mountains and lava flows
- Main routes
- Crusader and Byzantine invasions and raids
- Islamic counter-moves

One section of the huge fortified walls of Cairo Citadel looking south from the Burg al-Ramla or 'Sandy Tower' towards the Burg al-Imam. These towers and the intervening wall were erected between 1183 and 1207. They incorporate several very advanced features including vaulted passages inside the curtain wall. One of the stairways leading from the upper rampart to such a passage can be seen in the foreground. (David Nicolle photograph)

Turkish Anatolia and only a small part reached Syria. Others came directly by sea. Once assembled in Palestine the Second Crusade attacked Damascus instead of marching against the main threat in northern Syria. Even so they failed, being defeated by weak local forces and militias

Saladin

Salah al-Din Yusuf Ibn Ayyub was born in 1138 into the minor Kurdish military aristocracy. He was brought up in the service of Zangi, his father being governor of Baalbek. Saladin was educated in the typical manner of the Turco-Arab military aristocracy. He entered the service of Zangi's son Nur al-Din and accompanied his uncle on two expeditions to Egypt. Following the second successful expedition, Saladin became the wazir or chief minister of the last Fatimid Caliph. When the latter died in 1171 Saladin took over as governor of Egypt under the suzereinty of Nur al-Din of Aleppo. After the ruler of Aleppo died in 1174, Saladin gradually extended his control over most of what had been Nur al-Din's territory. Despite earlier and less successful clashes, Saladin's invasion of the Crusader Kingdom of Jerusalem resulted in overwhelming victory in 1187, including the reconquest of Jerusalem itself. Thereafter he held on to the Holy City despite Western Christendom's massive effort in the Third Crusade. He died in 1193. Pious and orthodox, an astute politician and an excellent military commander, Saladin was regarded as a pattern of chivalry by his Frankish foes and as an ideal ruler by many, though not all, in the Islamic world.

and Syrian-Turkish armies as well as political and military factions within the Fatimid Caliphate. In 1169 Nur al-Din's general Shirkuh seized Cairo and the Crusader army evacuated Egypt. That same year Shirkuh died and his nephew, Saladin, became not only Nur al-Din's governor and commander of the Syrian forces in Egypt, but also of the Fatimid army and navy. After ruthless purging and reorganisation these formed Saladin's first powerbase, to which he gradually added more troops including a significant force of slave-recruited mamluks.

The Crusader States seemed paralysed before this looming threat and when Nur al-Din and King Almaric of Jerusalem both died in 1174, Saladin added Damascus to his realm. Over the next few years Saladin extended his authority further, either by direct annexation or by obliging Nur al-Din's descendants to recognise his overlordship. At this stage Saladin's occasional brushes with the Crusader States seemed designed to improve his standing among his fellow

Richard I of England

Richard, called Coeur de Lion, was born in 1157, the third son of King Henry II. He became King of England in 1189, led a major contingent in the Third Crusade and married Berengaria of Navarre while in Cyprus, which he had conquered from the Byzantines. Richard defeated Saladin at Arsuf but failed to retake Jerusalem. Attempting to return home overland, he was imprisoned by Duke Leopold of Austria. Ransomed in 1194, King Richard returned home and fought King Philip Augustus of France in Normandy, being killed in 1199 while besieging Chaluz. Richard was regarded as one of the finest exponents of chivalry, handsome and physically brave but ostentatious. He spent barely six months in England as king, regarding it merely as a place to raise money. King Richard I was also a leading patron of *troubadours*, as his mother Eleanor of Aquitaine had been.

outside Damascus in 1148. The Second Crusade was, in fact, a fiasco which destroyed a potential alliance between the Crusader States and Damascus against Mosul and Aleppo. A few years later, in 1154, Nur al-Din added Damascus to his expanding domain.

Since the first attempt by King Almaric I of Jerusalem to take control of Egypt, the Muslim and Christian powers in Syria had hoped to annexe this wealthy and densely populated country. This resulted in a series of remarkable campaigns, involving Crusader

French sword, 1150–75. This is a very typical knightly weapon of the later 12th century. The pommel is a flattened nut shape while the *quillons* broaden towards their ends. Such a sword-hilt is shown in a great deal of art from this period, but usually appears in a chunkier, less delicate manner than the real weapon. The blade has a single broad *fuller* or groove down most of its length and also has a now unintelligible inlaid inscription. (Royer Collection, Paris, France)

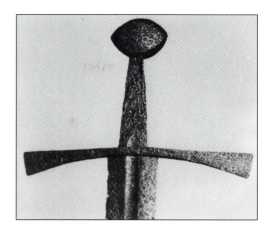

Muslims. He also retook the southern tip of Palestine; a victory which was presented as the 'freeing' of the Islamic pilgrim route from Egypt to the Holy Cities of Mecca and Medina, which was good for Saladin's credentials as a leader of the jihad. It also meant that communication between Saladin's two powerbases in Egypt and Syria, though difficult, was free from anything more serious than occasional Crusader raids.

In 1187 Saladin launched a major campaign against the Kingdom of Jerusalem. This, like the First Crusade, achieved greater success than Saladin probably expected. The Christian army was virtually annihilated at the battle of Hattin and Jerusalem was retaken along with almost all the Kingdom of Jerusalem and a considerable amount of other Crusader territory. This caused an even greater shock than had the fall of Edessa, and resulted in the Third Crusade. Emperor Frederick Barbarossa marched in 1189 but was drowned in Anatolia, only a small part of his army reaching Syria. Next year King Philip of France and King Richard of England set out by sea. Other European leaders were also involved in this huge enterprise but the results, though significant, were far less than might have been expected from a pan-European effort to reconquer the Holy Land. Even the famous battle of Arsuf was little more than a failed ambush from Saladin's point of view. Nevertheless, Saladin's army was exhausted by the time the Third Crusade ended. A rump Kingdom of Jerusalem was recreated, but without Jerusalem, and the great coastal port of Acre remained the effective capital of the Crusader east until its fall in 1291.

The emphasis of the Crusading movement in the Middle East now changed.

Increasingly it focused on breaking Islamic power in Egypt, which was the main threat to what remained of the Crusader States. Egypt was also accessible now that Western European domination of the Mediterranean was overwhelming; Cyprus, taken from the Byzantines during the Third Crusade, provided an excellent naval base.

During the 13th century the fate of the Crusader States became entangled in the rivalries of Western powers, most notably those of the German Empire and southern Italy. In fact the rulers of Sicily sometimes seemed to view the affairs of Jerusalem as part of their own ambitions to dominate the

Pope Innocent III
Lotario de'Conti de Segni was born in 1160 of a noble family. Vigorous, quick-witted and highly educated in theology and law at Paris and Bologna universities, Lotario had very elevated views of the Papacy. Unfortunately he tended to be hasty, arrogant, legalistic and what today might be termed a 'control freak'. Elected Pope in 1198 at the young age of 37 with the name of Innocent III, his tenure saw continued efforts to promote papal supremacy over temporal rulers, the suppression of heresies and support for Crusades. He is often regarded as the chief architect of the powerful Papacy of the 13th century.

The fortified port of Aigues Mortes was specially built as a powerful base in southern France from which to launch Crusading expeditions. Whether it was started by King Louis IX or dates entirely from the reign of King Philip the Fair is unclear, but most of the walls and towers clearly date from Philip's reign, 1285 to 1314. Today the seashore is some way away from the town, which is partly surrounded by reed marshes. (David Nicolle photograph)

entire Eastern Mediterranean. At the same time antipathy between Catholic Western Europe and Orthodox Eastern Europe was increasing. Such tensions, added to the declining authority of the Byzantine Emperors and the Venetian desire to control the region's trade, culminated in the

The Fourth Crusade attacks the port of Constantinople, as described in Villehardouin's Chronicle:

"The appointed time was now come and the knights went on board the transport ships with their war-horses. They were fully armed, with their helmets laced on, while the horses were covered with their armours and were saddled. All the other people who were of less importance in battle were in the larger ships. The galleys were also fully armed and made ready. The weather was fair and a little after dawn the Emperor Alexius (III) was waiting for them on the other side with a great army and with everything in order. Now the trumpets sounded and every galley took a

transport ship in tow so that they could reach the other side [of the Golden Horn] more quickly ... The knights came out of the transports and leapt fully armed into the sea up to their waists, helmets on their heads and spears in their hands. The good archers and the good crossbowmen, each in their units, scrambled ashore as soon as their ships touched the ground. At first the Greeks made a good resistance but when it came to the meeting of spears they turned their backs and fled, abandoned the shoreline ... Then the sailors began to open the doors of the transports, let down the ramps and took out the horses. The knights mounted and were marshalled in their correct divisions."

diversion of the Fourth Crusade against Constantinople. This led to the creation of a short-lived 'Latin Empire' of Constantinople and of several Latin-Crusader States in Greece, plus the emergence of Byzantine successor states in Epirus, Nicea and Trebizond. From then on effective military co-operation between Latin and Orthodox, Western and Eastern Christian states became difficult if not impossible. It was a turning point in the history of the Crusades.

The need to support new Latin-Crusader states in the Balkans also diverted resources away from the Middle Eastern Crusader States at a time when European enthusiasm for Crusading was in steep decline. Like virtually all the later Crusades, the Fifth

Crusade of 1218–21 was a government-led rather than popular movement. It started with relatively small-scale operations against neighbouring Islamic territory in Syria but then a bolder plan was devised. The Crusaders would attack Egypt itself but this time, with control of the Eastern Mediterranean, they could invade from the sea. Although the resulting campaign demonstrated the sophistication of Western European combined operations, it failed with the Crusader army surrendering to the forces of Saladin's nephew, al-Kamil, in 1221. The Sixth Crusade, led by the cultured but excommunicated Western Emperor Frederick II, was a diplomatic exercise rather than a military expedition and resulted in the peaceful transfer of Jerusalem to Crusader sovereignty in 1229. From then on the military, political and diplomatic situation of the Crusader States deteriorated both in Syria-Palestine and Greece. Small groups of Crusaders would arrive from the West, invariably conduct ineffective raids that merely annoyed neighbouring Islamic rulers, and then sail back to Europe. One of these led by Thibaut of Champagne, the King of

Clairmont Castle, now called Khlemoutsi Castle, built in 1220–23, was one of the most important fortresses in Crusader Greece. It defended the lands of the Villehardouin family, whose capital was at nearby Andravida, and consisted of an outer wall, the large eliptical inner ward, and a series of rooms and galleries including a chapel built against the outer wall. In most cases only their fireplaces remain. The keep, seen here on the right, was basically hexagonal with huge vaulted galleries around a central court. (Ian Meigh photograph)

Egyptian use of naft against the Crusaders outside the captured city of Dumyat, according to De Joinville's Chronicle:

"One night when we were guarding the *chas-chastiaus* the Saracens brought up an engine called a *pierrière* which they had not used before. They put Greek Fire into the sling of this engine. When my Lord Gautiers d'Escuiré, a good knight who was with me, said; 'Lords, we are in the greatest peril so far, for if they set fire to our towers and we are inside them, we are doomed and burned up. But if we leave these defences which we have been ordered to defend, we are dishonoured … So my advice is this. Every time they throw the fire at us, we drop on our elbows and knees, and pray to our Saviour to save us.' As soon as they threw their first shot, we threw ourselves on our elbows and knees as he had shown us. That first shot fell between the two chas-chastiaus. It fell right in front of us, where the army had been damming the river … The Greek Fire was hurled towards us like a large barrel of vinegar, and the tail of fire which came from it was as long as a large lance.
The noise it made as it came was like heaven's thunder, and it seemed as if a dragon was flying through the air. It also shed so much light … that one could see the camp as clearly as if it had been daytime."

Navarre, was graced with the title of the Seventh Crusade. It tried to take advantage of rivalry between Saladin's Ayyubid descendants who ruled in Cairo, Damascus and elsewhere. This resulted in an unsuccessful alliance with Damascus, a serious defeat near Gaza, a coup d'état in Cairo which placed a more effective Ayyubid Prince on the Egyptian throne, and Thibaut sailing home in disgust. Jerusalem was lost

Aerial view of Irbil taken in the early 1930s. Irbil was a major centre of military power and of culture in northern Iraq during the 12th and 13th centuries, particularly when Saladin's Turkish general Gökböri was the city's governor. When this photograph was taken, it had still not expanded far beyond the original circular walled hilltop medieval city. Even today, after being ravaged by Mongols and damaged in 20th-century wars, Irbil still has the beautifully decorated brick minaret of the Great Mosque built by Gökböri. (Flight Lieutenant Sharpe photograph. St Andrews University Library Photographic Collection, St Andrews, Scotland)

The famous but very damaged wall-painting at Cressac is unusual in illustrating specifically Crusader knights, French 12th century. The scene is believed to illustrate their defeat of Nur al-Din in the Buqaia valley in 1163. A 19th-century reproduction of this section of the wall-painting, made before it suffered further damage, shows that the little figure apparently seated behind one of the knight's shields, was playing a stringed instrument. Perhaps he represented the musicians who also accompanied some Crusader armies into battle. (*in situ* Protestant church, Cressac, France. David Nicolle photograph)

again in 1244, taken by an army of Khwarazmian military refugees called in by the Sultan of Egypt. Then, in alliance with the Egyptian army, they inflicted a crushing defeat on the Christians and their allies from Damascus at La Forbie, north of Gaza. It was the last time an army from the Crusader States challenged a comparable Islamic army in open battle.

In 1249 the Eighth Crusade led by King Louis IX of France was a more ambitious, better organised and better led expedition and once more was aimed at Egypt. The Crusaders landed at Dumyat on the eastern branch of the Nile, and marched upriver towards Cairo, as they had done previously. They again reached Mansura, named in commemoration of the defeat of the Fifth Crusade, and were again crushed in 1250.

Danishmandamah, originally written c.1245 for Sultan Kay Kawus II of Seljuk Rum, describing how Malik Danishmend fought a Christian knight named Tatis:

"The evil Tatis attacked Malik Danishmend with his lance; Malik parried with his shield. They fought on with blows of their lances, and because of the violence and the strength of these blows they burst the links which held their coat of mail and so, ring by ring, these tumbled to the ground ... The neighing of horses, the rattle of armour and harness, the clatter of swords, the crash of maces, the whistling of arrows, the twang of bows and the cries of warriors filled the air."

During the course of this Eighth Crusade a military coup in Egypt overthrew the Ayyubid Sultan and, after a complex transition period, replaced Saladin's descendants with a remarkable new form of government – the Mamluk Sultanate. Here the ruler was himself a soldier of slave-recruited origin. The state now existed to maintain the army while the army was

wholly dominated by soldiers of mamluk origin, mostly Turks from Central Asia or southern Russia. More immediately, this new Mamluk Sultanate faced a daunting array of challenges even after the defeat of the Eighth Crusade.

The Mongol Hordes under Genghis Khan and his descendants had already invaded the eastern Islamic world, raising visions in Europe of a potent new ally, which would join Christians in destroying Islam. Even after the Mongol invasion of Orthodox Christian Russia, followed by their terrifying rampage across Catholic Hungary and parts of Poland, many in the West still regarded the Mongols as potential allies. The Muslims, of course, recognised the Mongols as mortal foes. In 1258 Genghis Khan's grandson Hulegu conquered the sadly diminished city of Baghdad, killing its last 'Abbasid Caliph.

King Louis IX of France
Born in 1214, Louis came to the throne at the age of 12. Though generally conservative, his reign was a positive period in French history and also saw improved relations with England. Louis was a man of strong character, neither extravagant nor subservient to the Church. Nevertheless, he tried hard to establish peace among Christian rulers. Soldierly and brave, King Louis became obsessed by the idea of Crusade in his later years, and he died in 1270 while leading an expedition against Tunis. He was not only a pious man but was concerned that justice was available for all. The French king was canonised as St Louis in 1297.

Effigy of Othon de Grandson, Savoyard-Swiss early 14th century. Othon was one of those who survived the fall of the Crusader city of Acre to the Mamluks in 1291. He then continued his very successful career in the service of the English crown. His effigy dates from the early 14th century and the military equipment it illustrates, though old-fashioned, is shown in very interesting detail. Even the bulge caused by the knight's ears beneath the mail of his coif, and almost certainly a partially padded cloth coif beneath, has been accurately shown. (*in situ* Cathedral, Lausanne, Switzerland. David Nicolle photograph)

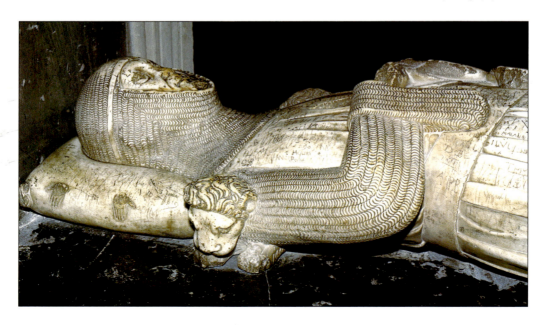

Krak des Chevaliers

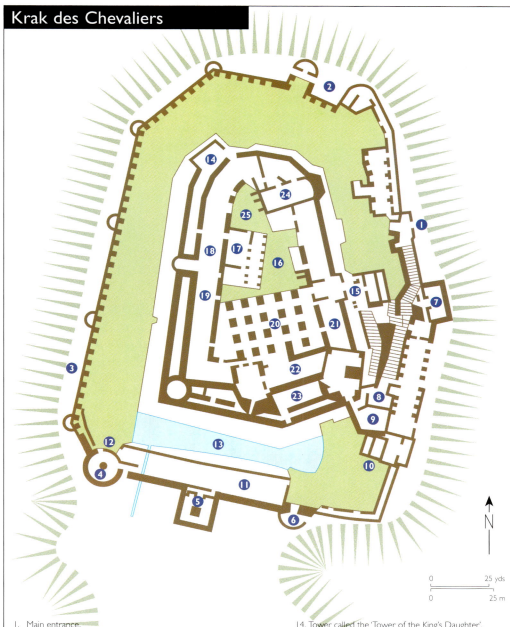

1. Main entrance.
2. Rock-cut secondary entrance between two towers.
3. Outer wall with machicolations.
4. Tower reconstructed by the Mamluk Sultan Baybars in 1271 AD.
5. Tower probably reconstructed by the Mamluk Sultan Qalawun in 1285 AD.
6. Small tower with a postern gate.
7. Large salient tower reconstructed by the Mamluks.
8. Entrance ramp.
9. Tower dominating the entrance ramp.
10. Haman (Turkish bath).
11. Long vaulted chamber.
12. Entrance stair to outer ward.
13. Water-filled moat.

14. Tower called the 'Tower of the King's Daughter'.
15. Tower protecting the entrance to the inner keep.
16. Inner courtyard which originally had a small spiral staircase to the roof of the castle.
17. Chapter House and Cloister.
18. Long vaulted chamber.
19. Long vaulted chamber.
20. Perhaps the Refectory.
21. Warehouse.
22. Warehouse used to store olive oil.
23. Small warehouse with oil-press.
24. Chapel (converted to a mosque after the Mamluk conquest).
25. Small courtyard with stairs (later addition) to the roof of the castle.

Carving of a demon loading a crossbow, French early 12th century. The demon spans or pulls back the string of the weapon by placing his feet on the arms of the bow, while apparently holding the arrow or bolt in his mouth. This was the earliest and most primitive method of loading a weapon which the Church and the feudal military elite still regarded as 'demonic' because it threatened the knight's supposed domination of warfare. (*in situ* cloisters of the church of St Pierre, Moissac, France. David Nicolle photograph)

Abu'l-'Abbas al-Nasir li-Din Allah
Born in 1158, the son and successor to the Caliph al-Mustadi', al-Nasir ruled as 'Abbasid Caliph of Baghdad from 1180 to 1225. He had been kept in virtual isolation by a father who feared his son would be corrupted by dangerous new ideas. His relations with his mother, a Turkish slave, were easier. Al-Nasir had to defend his position when he came to the throne but went on to revive the power and prestige of the Sunni 'Abbasid Caliphate, which had been in the shadow of secular rulers for centuries. This also resulted in a localised extension of Caliphal territory. Baghdad again became the focal point of the Sunni Islamic world and al-Nasir even tried to reunite the separated strands of Islam. The network of alliances which he formed destroyed the remnants of the Seljuk Sultanate in Iran in 1194, but unfortunately the Khwarazmshahs who replaced the Seljuks proved even more dangerous neighbours. Some sources even suggest that the Caliph al-Nasir called upon the Mongol leader Genghis Khan to attack the Khwarazmshah from the east. Certainly many Muslims in Syria and Egypt felt that the Caliph was more interested in eastern affairs than in the threat posed by the Crusaders. He died in 1225.

The following year he took Damascus before returning to Central Asia. But in 1260 the Mongol army which Hulegu had left to continue the conquest of Syria was itself defeated by the Mamluks at the battle of 'Ayn Jalut in Palestine. This was the first time that a major Mongol army had been defeated in open battle by a comparable Islamic force and was a turning point in the Mongol invasion of the Islamic world. Eventually the conversion of the Il-Khans (as the Mongol occupiers of Iran and Iraq were known) to Islam at the end of the 13th century meant that the struggle became one

between rival Muslim dynasties rather than between Muslims and alien outsiders.

Though the feeble Crusader States and occasional Crusading expeditions from the West were drawn in, the Crusaders were now little more than pawns in a greater game. For their part the Mamluk rulers of Egypt and Syria recognised that these European enclaves on their left flank were a strategic danger and so decided to remove them once and for all. Meanwhile the Crusader States were weakened by internal quarrels between those supporting this or that nominal king of Jerusalem, between rival Italian merchant

Arms and armour fragments from the ruins of the Great Palace in Istanbul (Constantinople), Byzantine 12th century. They were found in association with coins dating from the middle and later Comnenid period. Nevertheless, this military equipment is more typical of the western steppes in what are now the Ukraine and southern Russia than with what we know of Byzantine arms and armour. This is particularly true of the iron 'face-mask' visors, one of which has here been photographed from the inside. Perhaps they were used by Kipchaq Turkish mercenaries in Byzantine Imperial service. (Present whereabouts unknown. St Andrews University Library Photographic Collection)

republics in pursuit of trading advantages, and even between the great Military Orders of the *Templars* and the *Hospitallers*. Moreover, Mamluk raiders devastated the orchards, market gardens and sugar plantations close to the remaining Crusader cities and castles. One by one the latter fell. Most were razed but sometimes the Mamluks took over a Crusader castle for their own use, strengthening them still further.

In 1268 the Mamluks under Sultan Baybars devastated Antioch. In 1270 King Louis IX set out on Crusade once again but this time against Tunis in North Africa rather than to the Middle East. Nevertheless, it was another disaster, culminating in Louis' death. Next year a small force gathered in Syria under the leadership of Prince Edward of

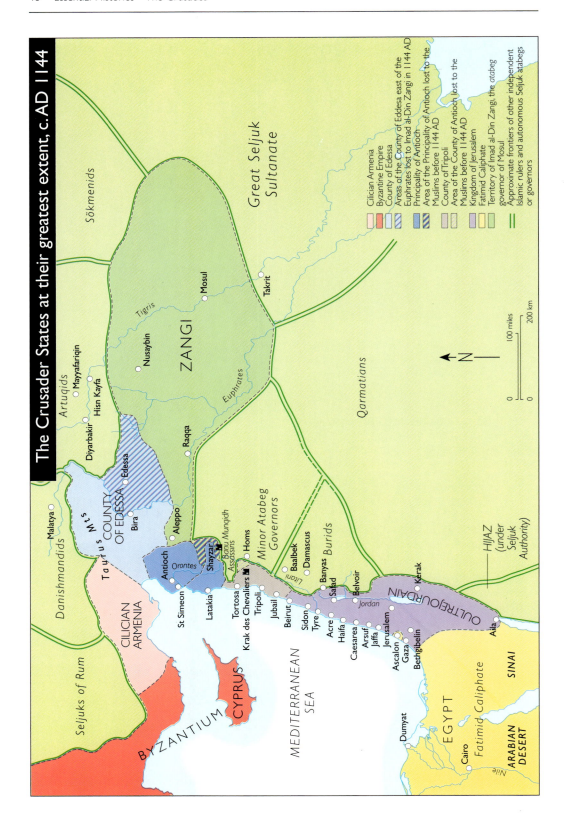

The Crusader States at their greatest extent, c.AD 1144

Danishmandids

Seljuks of Rum

Sökmenids

Artuqids

Mayyafariqin

Diyarbakir

Hisn Kayfa

Malatya

Tauus Mts

COUNTY OF EDESSA

Edessa

Bira

Aleppo

Banu Munqidh

Shayzar

Assassins

Orontes

Antioch

St Simeon

Latakia

CILICIAN ARMENIA

BYZANTIUM

CYPRUS

MEDITERRANEAN SEA

Krak des Chevaliers

Tortosa

Tripoli

Jubail

Beirut

Sidon

Tyre

Acre

Haifa

Caesarea

Arsuf

Jaffa

Ascalon

Gaza

Bethgibelin

Jerusalem

Homs

Baalbek

Damascus

Banyas

Safad

Belvoir

Jordan

Litani

Minor Atabeg Governors

Burids

OUTREJOURDAN

Kerak

Aila

HIJAZ (under Seljuk Authority)

ZANGI

Mosul

Takrit

Tigris

Nusaybin

Raqqa

Euphrates

Great Seljuk Sultanate

Qarmatians

Dumyat

Cairo

Nile

EGYPT

Fatimid Caliphate

SINAI

ARABIAN DESERT

N

0   100 miles
0   200 km

Cilician Armenia
Byzantine Empire
County of Edessa
Areas of the County of Edessa east of the Euphrates lost to Imad al-Din Zangi in 1144 AD
Principality of Antioch
Area of the Principality of Antioch lost to the Muslims before 1144 AD
County of Tripoli
Area of the County of Antioch lost to the Muslims before 1144 AD
Kingdom of Jerusalem
Fatimid Caliphate
Territory of Imad al-Din Zangi, the *atabeg* governor of Mosul
Approximate frontiers of other independent Islamic rulers and autonomous Seljuk atabegs or governors

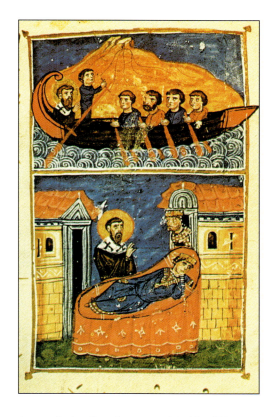

A war-galley in a Byzantine manuscript of the 12th century. A number of illustrations of Byzantine warships exist, and several give the vessels red-painted prows and sterns. Perhaps this was a form of identification that could be seen from a great distance. Otherwise the written sources suggest that it could be very difficult to identify friend from foe in Mediterranean naval warfare. (*Sermons of St. Gregory Nazianzus*, Monastery of Panteleimon, Mount Athos, Greece)

England, the future King Edward I, but it was too small, the Crusader States too anarchic and the Mamluk opposition too strong. The same year even the huge Hospitaller fortress of Krak des Chevaliers was lost.

For the rest of the 1270s Mamluk attention focused on their struggle with the Mongols, but in 1285 a new Sultan, Qalawun, was able to return to the task of defeating the Crusaders. His first target was the remnants of the County of Tripoli and what was in all but name a Hospitaller 'statelet' around Margat. Margat fell in 1285, Tripoli in 1289. The Crusader States were in their final extremity and desperate appeals for help produced some help from Western Europe. In 1290 a fleet of Venetian and Aragonese warships arrived with troops in what could be called the last Crusade, but it was already too little and too late.

In 1291 the Mamluk Sultan al-Ashraf Khalil, Qalawun's son, assembled a huge army, drawing in volunteers and professionals from Egypt and Syria, plus a formidable array of the best siege engines yet

Wall painting of warrior saints, Byzantino-Serb, c.1265. Occasionally Byzantine paintings of military saints show them without the usual antique armour. As a result they might look more like the Byzantine, Serbian or Bulgarian military elite of the time when they were painted. Here, for example, both men are armed with spears but the one on the left has a round shield while the saint on the right has a form of elongated or triangular shield. (*in situ* church, Sopocani Monastery, Serbia. David Nicolle photograph)

'Imad al-Din al-Isfahani on Saladin's last attempt to raise the siege of Acre:
    "It was said that one part of the [Crusader] defence was held by a Frank who seemed like a *jinni*, very agile and confident in the devil's help … He had taken his shield and made it into a shell for his body, but it became a target for arrows so that he soon resembled a hedgehog covered in spikes. The arrows remained stuck in his protection but could not penetrate it. This man was eventually killed when a bottle of Greek Fire (*naft*) was smashed against his 'shell.'"

Anon, Les Chétifs, *a late 12th-century French Crusade cycle that describes an army arrayed:*
    "See and note each knight mounted, each hauberk and each helmet and each shield in rows. Each lance tipped with steel and each blade fixed, and each fine war-horse in decorated harness, each good sword and each javelin pointed towards the foe, each war-axe resting upon a shoulder, the crossbows drawn, their arrows aimed."

devised. Their target was the great coastal city of Acre. The siege was bitter and only lasted seven weeks before the Mamluks broke in. The fall of Acre is usually seen as the end of the Crusades in the Holy Land with most of the remaining enclaves of Tyre, Beirut, Atlit, Tortosa and Haifa being abandoned before the Mamluks attacked. Sidon resisted for a while but was then evacuated.

All that remained was Jubail (in what is now Lebanon) and the little Syrian offshore island of Ruad. At Jubail the local lord, Peter Embriaco, had already submitted to Mamluk suzereinty and seems to have retained his lordship for several years, his successors perhaps converting to Islam and being absorbed into the Mamluk state. The Templars

clung to Ruad until ousted by the Mamluks in 1302. Cilician Armenia survived, initially as an ally of the Mongol Il-Khans, until the Mamluks and Anatolian Turks joined forces to crush this potentially dangerous outpost in 1375. The Crusader Kingdom of Cyprus lasted far longer and served as a base from which Western European fleets launched naval raids – sometimes graced with the title of Crusades – against the Mamluk Sultanate during the 14th century.

Although the First Crusade included non-combatants, the success of the movement naturally depended upon its fighting men. The bulk of the cavalry came from the lower military elite or knights. Their equipment reflected their wealth and status, which varied considerably though the possession of adequate arms and horses was a basic requirement. Their primary weapons were the lance and the sword, the former usually used in the *couched* manner where it was firmly tucked beneath the upper-right arm and pointed directly ahead. This meant that an individual horseman could only attack an opponent immediately in front of him. But the couched lance was not intended to be an individual weapon, rather it was the weapon of a close-packed line of horsemen or conrois in which individuals were trained to act as a co-ordinated team. The knight's sword was a secondary weapon, to be drawn and used in the *mêlée* after a charge had been delivered, or in a defensive situation or when the lance was inappropriate.

Less is known about Western European infantry at the time of the First Crusade but they were not a despised rabble. In fact they would have included professional foot soldiers or sergeants, plus part-time militiamen from the cities and ordinary volunteers. Nor should the capabilities of the

Standard-bearers and musicians in an Islamic army, as illustrated in one of the best known Iraqi manuscripts from the early 13th century. Flags, banners and military bands played a major role in Middle Eastern warfare, and had done so since well before the Islamic era. Nevertheless, the Muslims brought them to a fine art with a great variety of forms and shapes of banner, and special corps of drummers, trumpeters and so on. They not only helped to maintain morale but assisted in the identification of units and communication between commanders and their troops. ("Maqamat of al-Hariri", Ms. Arabe 5847, f.19, Bibliothèque Nationale, Paris, France)

Ceramic fragment showing a Fatimid Egyptian infantryman, Egypt 11th–12th centuries. This damaged fragment of lustreware ceramic provides one of the most interesting existing illustrations of an Islamic Middle Eastern foot soldier from the early Crusader period. As in other sources, he protects his head with a bulky turban, is armed with a broad-bladed spear and a kite-shaped shield. His left arm and shoulder are given a different pattern to the rest of his costume, perhaps suggesting that a mail hauberk is worn beneath a fabric outer garment. (Study Collection, Victoria & Albert Museum, London, England. David Nicolle photograph)

latter be dismissed at a time when most men knew how to use some sort of weapon. By the end of the 11th century such infantry included crossbowmen as well as ordinary archers, an increase in the importance of the crossbow being the most significant feature of 12th-century Western European warfare.

There were no real changes in knightly cavalry warfare except for a refinement of existing tactics. Even the changes in cavalry equipment largely reflected the threat from crossbows. In the Crusader Middle East, Islamic archery was a comparable threat. As a result, knightly armour grew notably heavier and more all-covering, while horse armour was also adopted. The resultant increasing weight must have been a major factor in the use of larger horses, since a horse needs to be heavy to carry weight.

Western European infantry tactics, like those of the cavalry, were refined rather than changed and the role of foot soldiers remained essentially defensive. In open battle or while marching through hostile territory infantry protected cavalry by forming a defensive perimeter or line. From such formations the cavalry could launch the charges, which remained the only real offensive tactic in the Crusader armoury. The other major role of foot soldiers was, of course, in siege warfare. In this situation they and any siege engineers or labourers would be led and supported by the knightly elite. Infantry armour was essentially the same as that of the cavalry, though lighter and generally lacking leg protection and the massive forms of vision-restricting helmets adopted by many European cavalry in the later 12th century.

Infantry weapons were more varied and often more complex than those of the cavalry. The crossbow, like the composite bow, which was used in Italy, the Crusader States and other parts of the Christian Mediterranean world, was a sophisticated weapon. By the late 13th century its power increased yet further. In addition to spears, swords and daggers, foot soldiers wielded an extraordinary array of pole-arms, often reflecting their place of origin. These often included thrusting points, hacking blades, armour-penetrating horizontal points and sometimes even hooks to pull horsemen from their saddles. The shields used by foot soldiers similarly ranged from small hand-held *bucklers* to massive *mantlets,* which could be rested on the ground to form a fixed 'shield-wall'.

The military equipment of Islamic armies was more complex, reflecting a wider and more varied military heritage. To some extent this was also true of the Byzantine arms. In military technological and tactical matters the 12th- to 13th-century Middle East had a heritage going back to the Romano-Byzantine and Sassanian Persian past, added to which were the neglected traditions of the Arabian peninsula and those of Turco-Mongol

Central Asia, plus some influence from Mediterranean Europe. These had been amalgamated and refined during the 7th to the 11th centuries, resulting in the most sophisticated military heritage of the age. This military heritage was also a literate one in which military manuals were widely available.

A common image of Islamic armies consisting almost entirely of cavalry is very misleading. In reality these forces reflected their places of origin, patterns of recruitment and the military heritage of their ruling elite. None relied solely on horse-archers, though 12th- to 13th-century Islamic cavalry did include many such Turks. The professional soldiers, whether of mamluk or freeborn

Turkish weapons, 10th–12th centuries. An assortment of typical Turco-Mongol or Central Asian weapons fragments were found during archaeological excavations at the Citadel of Kuva. This area, close to the frontier with China, became the heartland of the Kara-Khanid Sultanate which rivalled the Seljuks for the domination of the north-eastern provinces of the Islamic world during the Crusader period. The weapons themselves, including parts of daggers, arrowheads and spearheads, would have been identical to those used by Seljuk warriors both here in Transoxania, in Iran and in Syria. (Archaeological Museum, Kuva, Uzbekistan. David Nicolle photographs)

origin, were generally trained to use spears, swords, maces, daggers and bows. The latter could be shot in the Central Asian long-range harassment manner, at close range in wheeling charges, or by men in static or slow-moving ranks.

It has been suggested that, to some degree, the success of the First Crusade resulted from a decline in battlefield discipline and skill on the part of this traditional Islamic military elite, while the ultimate expulsion of the Crusaders reflected a steady revival in their capabilities. It is certainly true that the fearsome Mamluk armies which finally destroyed the Crusader States were not using fundamentally new tactics, organisation, arms or armour. On the contrary they had much in common with the best Middle Eastern Islamic armies of the pre-Crusader period. What did change was the status of infantry, which slumped from the 11th to 14th centuries.

The weapons used by Islamic troops were not wholly different from those of the Crusaders. Initially most swords were straight, since the curved Central Asian sabre was still a new phenomenon in the 11th century. Muslim horsemen made more use of daggers in close combat than did their Western opponents, most notably the large *khanjar,* which might better be described as a short sword. Even the composite bow of wood, sinew and horn construction was not so different from that seen in Byzantium, southern Italy and the Iberian peninsula. What was different was a relatively new Turkish or Turco-Mongol form of composite bow of which the 'ears' or tips were shorter, thicker, stiffer and had a regularly recurved shape. It demanded greater strength, and perhaps more intensive training, but was more suited to use on a moving horse.

Where armour was concerned Islamic armies could draw upon more varied technology than their Western opponents. What they lacked was the abundance of iron which was already giving Western Europe a strategic advantage. Consequently the mail armour and iron helmets seen in both the Middle East and Europe were, in the former case, supplemented by iron and bronze *lamellar* cuirasses plus highly effective defences made of quilted material, hardened leather and even wood. The Middle East's

Part of a collection of bows and other archery equipment from northern Iraq, Syria or south-eastern Turkey, 12th–13th centuries. The date of this remarkable collection of arms, armour and horse-harness has been confirmed by carbon-dating tests. The hand bows are all of composite construction, exactly as described in the technical manuals of the period. They also appear to be of various sizes, strengths or draw weights. This again was typical of the Islamic Middle East, where all but the finest bows were manufactured in a mass-production manner, in three standardised strengths to suit the age or ability of the archer. (Private collection)

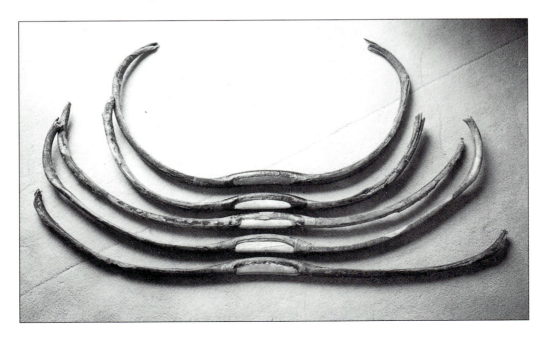

so-called 'soft armours' utilising cotton, silk, wool and other forms of impact-absorbing padding would be widely copied in Western Europe, but the Islamic world's varied forms of hardened leather defences only seem to have influenced the armours of Byzantium, Italy and the Iberian peninsula.

It has recently been argued convincingly that much of the elite cavalry of the wealthier Middle Eastern Islamic states rode larger horses than did the great majority of First Crusaders. Though professional mamluk cavalry used the couched lance in a similar manner to their Crusader opponents, this was not their main style of combat. Consequently their saddles did not develop the remarkably tall *pommels* and *cantles* seen in medieval Europe. In fact the traditional Middle Eastern military saddle was closer to the so-called 'cowboy saddle' of the American West. Horse armour of quilted felt, mail, scale or lamellar construction had always been known in the Islamic world but was restricted to the wealthiest states and a specific form of cavalry. These were usually elite horse-archers whose role was to cover

The so-called 'Baptistere de St Louis' is in reality a fine Egyptian or Syrian bronze basin inlaid with silver, gold and copper. In addition to scenes of Mamluk courtly life and ceremonial there are scenes of cavalry combat. Most of the horsemen appear to be unarmoured, though one has a full lamellar cuirass with a mail aventail across his face. In reality all the other fighting men probably wear mail lined by fabric-covered and padded *kazaghgands*, as described in Arabic written sources from this period. (Musée du Louvre, Paris, France)

the flanks and the withdrawal of close-combat cavalry.

Throughout the history of the Middle East until modern times, very few battles were fought in the desert. Almost all campaigns took place in the settled regions of the Nile Valley, Nile Delta, the *Fertile Crescent* from southern Palestine to southern Iraq, in neighbouring semi-arid steppe regions, or in the relatively sparsely populated regions of Anatolia and Iran. These were not only the regions most worth conquering or defending but they also contained the cities that served as focal points for trade. Furthermore, pre-modern armies were not really capable of operating in true desert. As a result the First

and subsequent Crusades operated in much these same agricultural, urban or semi-desert environments. Even the previously unstoppable Mongols found that their style of campaigning was severely limited by the dry Middle Eastern environment.

Other climatic features also played a part. In many parts of the Middle East the summer was too hot for effective fighting, and the autumn or winter either too wet in Syria or too cold in Anatolia and Iran. Horses needed to be fattened, crops gathered, mountain passes opened, the annual Nile flood to rise and fall. Even the monsoons of the Indian Ocean may have had an influence, through seasonal maritime trade, on the tax revenues of the Egyptian government. The health of Middle Eastern populations, including military elites, was similarly influenced by variable weather as it impacted on food levels and the spread of contagion. Infectious diseases tended to hit rural populations harder than nomadic ones, urban more than rural and settler or foreign groups – including newly arrived military elites – more than indigenous peoples. In fact few periods of were armed forces so dependent on ecological factors.

Stucco plaque showing armoured cavalrymen jousting or in combat, Iran 12th–13th centuries. The two men are very similarly equipped, both having a small form of *jawshan* lamellar cuirass over their chests. However, the horseman on the left also has a long cloth over his pointed hat or more probably helmet. This is given to elite guard figures or courtiers in other sources, and perhaps serves the same function here. (inv. 54.29, Art Museum, Seattle, USA)

From the section on armour in a military treatise written for Saladin by Muria Ibn 'Ali Muria al-Tarsusi:

"The *jawshan* is made by the Persians and is made of small plates of iron or horn or leather. One fashions the plates ... bound with gut, hollowed out and placed one over the other. The *kazghandah* was invented by those who became Arabs *[meaning the largely Semitic peoples who adopted Arabic during the early centuries of Islamic history]*. It is made of fine mail coats which are covered by quilted garments of silk and padding. Some use brocade or other decorated material."

Brothers in arms; two crusaders; two fursan

An Anglo-Norman crusader

Pagan Peverel was an Anglo-Norman knight who took part in the First Crusade, but like so many other participants this formed only a small part of his career. Pagan was probably the third son of Ranulph Peverel who, according to one story, made his fortune by marrying one of Duke William of Normandy's Saxon concubines. His eldest brother may even have been the Duke's illegitimate child. While Pagan's brothers made good marriages and became important men, he became a soldier and accompanied Duke Robert of Normandy on Crusade. He probably took over as one of Robert's standard-bearers following the death of Roger de Barnevilla outside Antioch. Pagan may also have participated in the Duke's raid on the Fatimid headquarters during the battle of Ascalon.

Pagan then returned to England, where he found favour with King Henry I, though probably more for his loyalty to the Norman ducal family than for his prowess on Crusade. According to the *Liber Memorandum Ecclesie de Barnewelle*, Pagan Peverel was 'a member of the King's household, an oustanding soldier ... and praiseworthy above all the nobles of the kingdom in matters of warfare'. In 1105 he was granted the manor of Shefford in Berkshire but five years later had a serious

Shayzar castle, village and watermill with the River Orontes. Shayzar in central Syria was the birthplace of Usamah Ibn Munqidh and was the centre of an 11th–12th century mini-state ruled by Usamah's family, the Banu Munqidh. It was right on the frontier of Islamic territory in Syria, with Crusader-held Afamiya to the north, an Ismail or 'Assassin' mini-state in the mountains to the west beyond which lay further Crusader territory. Only to the south and east lay normal Islamic territory, and this was held by local Turco-Seljuk governors who were often at loggerheads with the Banu Munqidh. (David Nicolle photograph)

St. George on a painted icon panel made in the Crusader States, probably in the late 13th century. Not only is this painting almost undamaged, but it also illustrates the warrior saint equipped in what is almost certainly the same manner as those *turcopole* light cavalry who served in the armies of the Crusader States. He has a spear, a relatively small round shield, a short-sleeved mail shirt and a box-style quiver identical to those used by Islamic horse-archers. His saddle is, however, typically Western European. The identity of the kneeling woman who kisses St George's foot is unknown, but she was probably the donor. Her costume also appears to be more Western European in style than Orthodox or Byzantine. (St Catherine's Monastery, Egypt)

quarrel with Ramsey Abbey over the possession of two villages, Stowe and Gretton. The King ordered a public trial of the two claims. Pagan lost and, according to the somewhat biased *Miracles of St Ivo*, he and his companions subsequently suffered a number of divinely ordained accidents. Pagan Peverel died after 1133, his son William then going on Crusade and dying in Jerusalem in 1147.

The servant of the king

Othon de Grandson was from the middle ranks of the feudal elite and his career is unusually well recorded. Born in 1238, the eldest son of Pierre, lord of Grandson in Savoy in what is now western Switzerland, Othon was considered to be destined for great things. He was probably brought up on stories of the Crusades since his grandfather had died in the Holy Land. He and his brother went to England to be educated in the royal households around 1247. Othon soon became a valuable man and seems to have been a companion of Prince Edward, the future King Edward I. In fact Othon accompanied Edward on Crusade to Tunisia and Palestine in 1270, being credited with saving the Prince's life by sucking out the poison from an assassin's dagger. He certainly remained one of Edward's must trusted men.

As King of England, Edward planned to go on Crusade again and to that end sent Othon de Grandson to do some diplomatic groundwork in 1290. As a result this Savoyard knight found himself in Acre when the final Mamluk attack came. Some sources say Othon fought bravely until resistance collapsed, while others claim he deserted his post. He certainly escaped with the money that Edward had entrusted to him, while losing his own possessions. Othon de Grandson spent the rest of his career serving the English crown, taking part in wars in Scotland and France and becoming Warden of the Channel Islands. Nevertheless, he died at the age of 90 only 50 miles from his birthplace, and was buried in Lausanne Cathedral.

Ambroise in his Itinerarium Peregrinorum, *on how the weather made things hard for the Third Crusade:*
    "When the arrangements were complete our men set out for the castle of Bayt Nuba, but the rain and hail was so heavy that many pack animals died. It pulled out tent pegs, drowned the horses and spoiled the bacon and biscuits. Weapons and armour got so rusty that a lot of hard work was needed to restore them to their previous condition. Clothes fell to pieces in the damp and men suffered from this unexpectedly bad weather."

An Arab cavalier

We only know about Jum'ah al-Numayri because he was the friend and military mentor of Usamah Ibn Munqidh and is frequently mentioned in Usamah's memoirs. These make it clear that Jum'ah was a highly rated and experienced cavalryman in the little garrison-army of Shayzar in central Syria. He was an Arab soldier who, as his name indicates, came from the *Banu Numayr* tribe. This had played a major military role in Syrian affairs for hundreds of years. In the 10th century their stronghold was the Harran area. During the 11th century the Banu Numayr also dominated the cities of Raqqa and Saruj, briefly being the independent rulers of this region. The Banu Numayr then played a major role resisting the Seljuk Turkish conquest of northern Syria and by the end of the 11th century were allies of Usamah's tribe or family, the Banu Munqidh.

Several men with the name al-Numayri served in Shayzar including Jum'ah's son Mahmud, but Jum'ah was the most senior. Usamah described him as: 'Our leading cavalryman and our most experienced soldier.' Usamah also recalled there was a knight in the neighbouring Crusader garrison at Afamiyah, his name being

'Badrhawa' (possibly Peter something). This Badrhawa was one of the enemy's most valiant men and used to say: 'Perhaps one day I shall meet Jum'ah in single combat.' Meanwhile Jum'ah used to say: 'Perhaps one day I shall meet Badrhawa in combat.' But they never did meet, because the Frank was killed by a lion while riding to Antioch. Usamah's memoirs contain numerous accounts of Jum'ah's character and exploits. One in particular sheds a fascinating light on the concern for personal honour and reputation among the elite Muslim cavalry

Carving of a fully armoured figure on a horse, Syria 12th century. The huge but largely ruined bridge at Ain Diwar was made in the 12th or very early 13th centuries. It once spanned the River Tigris, though this has since moved a few hundred metres to the east. Although the bridge is known as an important example of Islamic civil engineering from the Crusader era, its carvings never seem to have been published in detail. They illustrate astrological figures. This particular panel has a cavalryman riding side-saddle, presumably for iconographic reasons, and wearing a full-length lamellar jawshan cuirass over a long-sleeved mail dir' or hauberk. His face has been defaced but the sides of his head show that he also had a mail coif or perhaps an aventail attached to a low-domed round helmet. (in situ Ain Diwar bridge near Malkiyah, Syria. David Nicolle photograph)

of this period. Jum'ah, it seems, was terribly upset after being wounded by a younger and less experienced Kurdish horseman in the rival army of Hamah. The youngster was named Sarhank Ibn Abi Mansur. Later in the same battle Jum'ah went off on his own, then returned laughing, announcing that he had hit Sarhank while the latter was surrounded by his comrades and had then himself escaped unscathed.

The loyal Turk

Muzaffar al-Din Gökböri, whose name means 'Blue Wolf' in Turkish, came from a powerful Turkish family. His father was a Seljuk governor of Irbil in northern Iraq and became a loyal follower of Zangi, the first Muslim ruler to roll back the Crusader advance. Gökböri served Nur al-Din and supposedly became titular governor of Harran at the age of 14. In 1175 he commanded part of the Aleppo-Mosul army against Saladin at the battle of Hama. But Nur al-Din's inheritance was fragmenting and Gökböri recognised that Saladin was the

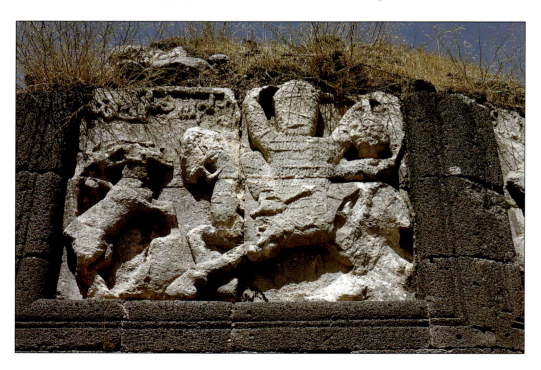

The remarkable array of 12th- to early 14th-century Syrian or Iraqi arms, armour and horse-harnesses which still awaits full publication includes several almost complete cuirasses. They are constructed of loops of hardened leather shaped to fit around the front or back of the wearer's body. Each is painted a colourful pattern and is made of several layers of thinner leather sewn and glued together. Each loop was then attached to its neighbours with leather straps on the inside. (Private collection)

rising star. He therefore invited Saladin to invade the Zangid lands north-east of the River Euphrates. Saladin attacked in 1182 and a year or so later gave Gökböri the towns of Edessa and Sumaysat as his reward. Gökböri also married one of Saladin's sisters, al-Sitt Rabia Khatun.

In 1185 some of Saladin's advisers accused the Turk of disloyalty and suggested executing him. Instead Saladin confiscated two of Gökböri's towns but allowed him to remain in his service. During Saladin's great victory at Hattin in 1187 Gökböri lived up to his reputation for standing firm while others quailed and so Saladin gave the Turk his father's original governorate around Irbil. There the great warrior also showed himself to be an enthusiastic patron of learning and

the arts. Gökböri is also said to have been the first Islamic ruler to encourage the previously unofficial Mawlid al-Nabi (Birthday of the Prophet Muhammad) festivities, perhaps in imitation of the Christmas celebrations held by Irbil's large Christian community. At the age of almost 80 Gökböri and his men joined those of the Caliph of Baghdad to shadow the Mongols who were now ravaging Iran. He fell ill during the campaign and returned home to Irbil, where he died in June 1233.

Baha' al-Din Ibn Shaddad in his Al-Nawadir al-Sultaniyah, *describing the Third Crusade as it marched south along the coast:*

"The enemy was formed in order of battle, the infantry drawn up in front of the cavalry, firm like a wall and every foot soldier wore a coat of thick felt and a coat of mail so strong that our arrows (shot from a distance) made no impression on them. But they shot at us with their great crossbows, wounding the Muslims' horses and their riders."

The impact of the Crusades on the Mediterranean and beyond

The economic impact of two centuries of Crusading warfare upon some parts of Europe was considerable. In many other areas, however, this impact was negligible. While in countries such as France, Germany and England the need to raise money to finance the Crusades did play some role in the development of government financial systems, it was only in Italy that the economic impact of the Crusades was really important. Even here the events of the 12th and 13th centuries were only part of the longer history of the trading relationship between the Italian states and their Islamic neighbours to the south and east, and their Graeco-Byzantine neighbours in the Balkans. Amalfitan merchants were present in Egypt well before the First Crusade and Italian seamen were already well on their way to achieving naval domination throughout the

The simple or folk art of 12th-century medieval Western Europe is often neglected by both art historians and those who study military technology. Here such a simple carved figure almost certainly represents a Crusader armed with a sword, largely lost when the top of this baptismal font was damaged, and carrying a large kite-shaped shield with a cross. (*in situ* parish church, Thorpe Arnold, England. David Nicolle photograph)

Mediterranean. By the fall of Acre at the end of the 13th century Italians not only dominated almost every corner of the Mediterranean but the Black Sea as well.

Economic links between Egypt and Sicily continued even after the Norman conquest of previously Muslim-ruled Sicily and trade links between Egypt and southern Italy as a whole were only briefly interrupted by the First Crusade. Further north, in Genoa and perhaps Pisa, trade links increased significantly during the 12th century, despite the supposedly deep-seated antagonism

Siena Cathedral is perhaps the biggest and most striking example of the use of black and white horizontal striped masonry as a form of decoration. It almost certainly reflected ideas brought back from the Islamic world and was built between 1196 and the early 14th century. (David Nicolle photograph)

An official letter from a Fatimid government official found in the Cairo Geniza or synagogue document store. It was addressed to the Caliph al-Amir (1101–30) and concerned Italian merchants who had brought a cargo of timber, probably to Alexandria:

"In the name of God, the Compassionate, the Merciful. The benedictions of God and His blessings. His increasing benefactions and most excellent peace and greetings be upon our Master and Lord, the 'Imam al-Amir bi-Akham Allah, Commander of the Faithful and his pure ancestors and noble descendants, benedictions that should last and remain until the Day of Judgement. This slave kisses the earth before the noble and exalted prophetical presence, may God double its light and may God extol its beacon. He reports the continued arrival of the Rum (Western European) merchants who come bringing timber and whose arrival this slave had reported. They are named: Sergius the son of Constantine, and S-r—ula the son of H—l-m, and Grasso the son of Leo the Amalfitan, and the Ruah(?), and Bon S-n-yun the Genoese, and their companions who are with them. They say that up to the time of this slave's writing it has not been established ... the timber ... reached them ... [end of the surviving page]."

Fulcher of Chartres on the perils facing ships linking the Crusader States to the West:

"Many are the troubles which, God willing or permitting, meet those sailing at sea. Sometimes the anchor breaks loose, sometimes a sailyard or the carved ornamental stern is broken, or the cables part ... Many ships are accustomed to run into danger in the Gulf of Adalia. Here the winds blow in violently from all sides, down the mountains into the valleys to be deflected through gorges and converging into a whirlwind in the Gulf. If sometimes the mariners meet a pirate ship they are robbed and pitilessly ruined. But those who suffer this for the love of God, will they ever be disappointed in His rewards?"

One of the most highly visible examples of the way in which later medieval Western European architecture was influenced by ideas brought back from the Crusades was in the use of black and white stone as a form of striped decoration; usually combining white limestone with dark grey volcanic basalt, which had been seen in the Middle East for many centuries. The Mausoleum Mosque of Shaykh Reslan in Damascus, built in the 12th century, is a particularly dramatic example. (David Nicolle photograph)

The German pilgrim Theoderich describes the Hospital of St John in Jerusalem in 1169:
"Unless he has had the opportunity of seeing it with his own eyes, no one can credibly explain how beautiful its buildings are, how abundantly it is supplied with rooms, beds and other material to be used for the poor and sick, how abundantly it has the means to refresh the poor, how devoutly it labours to support the needy. In fact we walked through this palace and were quite unable to discover the true number of those sick people who were lying there, but we saw ourselves that the beds alone numbered more than one thousand."

between Christendom and Islam epitomised by the Crusades. The role of Crusader States themselves in this pattern of trade was not as important as might have been expected, as they served more like colonial outposts or trading bases than economic units in their own right. As the Crusader States in both Syria-Palestine and in southern Greece shrank in territory and power, they became increasingly dependent upon outside supplies as well as military support. As a result southern Italy became a significant source of such things as food and horses. Even the fact that the Military Orders of the Templars, Hospitallers and *Teutonic Knights* also played a major role in supplying the Crusader States during the 13th century can be misleading. These Military Orders may have had their headquarters in the Crusader States, but their real economic power and influence was rooted in Western Europe. Meanwhile on land Italian merchants also played a major role in trade between Western Europe, much of Eastern Europe including Russia, those Islamic lands open to European merchants, and as far afield as China. While it would be an exaggeration to say that the

Crusades encouraged trading contact between Western Europe and the Islamic World, via Italian merchant 'states' such as Venice, Genoa, Pisa, Ancona and others, Crusading warfare rarely – and indeed only briefly – hindered trade across the religious frontier. Even Acre itself, effectively the capital of the Crusading Kingdom of Jerusalem from the late 12th century onwards, formed a vital link in this economic network. Indeed, 13th-century Acre has been described as an essential 'base' in a theoretically illegal trade in strategic goods including timber, weaponry and so on, between Venice and Egypt.

In purely financial terms the Crusades did stimulate banking and credit systems, with special regulations and structures being developed to enable individual Crusaders and their leaders to finance themselves and their armies. However, these financial systems were developing of their own accord, and the significance of the Crusades in particular remains a matter of debate. During the 12th century it had probably been the Church, and more specifically the monasteries, who had benefited from

A piratical contract made in Genoa in 1251:

"We, Guglielmo Mallone and Simonetto, brothers ... have received ... from you, Pietro Polpo de Mari, £250 Genoese ... for the voyage on which we are prepared to sail as corsairs in our ship, which is called *The Lion*, in order to win profit from the enemies of Holy Church ... if we make with the said ship a profit up to the amount of £3,000, we will give back to you the said loan and in addition £50 in every £100 in virtue of profit and gain from the said loan."

The seven-arched facade of al-Aqsa Mosque, facing the Dome of the Rock on the Temple Mount in Jerusalem, was built in 1217/18 by Saladin's nephew, al-Malik Mu'azzam, who was then the Ayyubid governor of Syria. This was between the first and second Crusader occupations of the Holy City. The architecture, though Islamic, shows considerable European influence in its three central porches. The Crusaders themselves regarded the main building, the earliest part of which dates from the early 8th century, as the Temple of Solomon and used it as the headquarters of the Military Order of the Templars. (David Nicolle photograph)

members of the European military aristocracy making grants of land in return for cash. In the 13th century, however, the whole question of financial planning and the amassing of adequate resources for huge overseas military expeditions became a major problem for Crusading leaders such as King Louis IX and Emperor Frederick II. In the event Louis and France proved to be much more efficient than Frederick and his ramshackle Empire in Germany and Italy.

Meanwhile the economic impact of the Crusades was almost entirely negative for the Byzantine Empire, which was, in any case, in economic decline. The Byzantines lost control not only of their neighbouring seas and the wealthy trade routes, but also

Woodblock printed paper, perhaps originally used as a textile design, found in the ruins of Fustat, Egypt 11th–12th centuries. It is not generally known that printing was widespread in the medieval Islamic world. Although this was done in the same manner as in China, using a single carved piece of wood rather than movable type, it was nevertheless an example of the technological sophistication of those countries which faced the Crusaders. (inv. Ms. 15005, Museum of Islamic Art, Cairo, Egypt. David Nicolle photograph)

eventually over their own domestic economy. This catastrophic decline had several causes, of which the Crusades were, however, only a minor part. Once again it was the Italians who largely inherited the wealth of the Byzantine Empire's foreign trade, while the Turks would eventually inherit both Byzantine territory and, of course, its domestic economy.

The impact of the Crusades upon the Islamic world was minimal and localised. Indeed, the whole Crusading episode was of far less importance to the Islamic world than is generally recognised. The Crusaders and the States that they established in the Middle East were more of an irritation than a real threat. The Islamic Middle East's trade with Europe had in any case been of secondary importance compared with trade to the east and perhaps even south. Trading links with Mediterranean Europe were rapidly re-established and while Europe's Papacy continued to fulminate against such links, the rulers of countries such as Egypt usually gave it their full support. Even the catastrophe of the

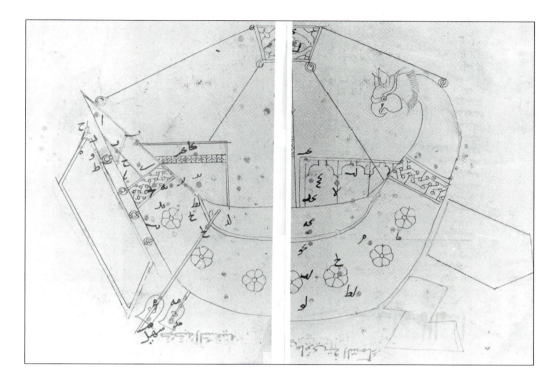

The star constellation Argo is usually shown in a very stylised manner in medieval manuscripts. Nevertheless, some Islamic astrological treatises include interesting details of hull construction and rigging. This example painted in Egypt in 1130/31 even has a hinged rudder long before such a device is supposed to have reached the Mediterranean. The artist was probably working from a verbal description, since the rudder looks very impractical. Since hinged stern rudders were certainly being used by Chinese ships, perhaps the description came from a Muslim sailor who had travelled across the Indian Ocean or beyond and had seen such a thing. Perhaps a Chinese merchant ship even reached Egypt or Iraq, and perhaps some Islamic shipbuilders in these eastern waters were already experimenting with the idea. (*Suwar al-Kawakib*, Ms. Ahmad III.3493, Topkapi Library, Istanbul, Turkey)

Mongol invasions in the 13th century ended up in having some economic benefit. Those areas most badly damaged by the passage of Mongol armies never recovered, but in broader terms the establishment of the so-called Mongol World Empire stretching from the South China Sea to Eastern Europe greatly facilitated long-distance trade between Europe and the Islamic world on one hand and China on the other.

The Crusades had virtually no impact on Western European society, except in certain very specific areas. The military aristocratic elite were influenced by Crusading ideals, while many Italian merchants and bankers grew wealthy as a result of the Crusades, but for the overwhelming majority of the ordinary people of Western Europe the Crusades were no more than interesting and exciting events which took place far, far away.

For the ordinary people of the Byzantine world the Crusades were often a far more immediate affair. Several large Crusading armies marched across Byzantine territory, often doing considerable damage as they went, while the Fourth Crusade targetted the Byzantine capital of Constantinople itself. In general, however, the impact of the Crusades and Crusading warfare was as localised as was almost all medieval warfare. Although the political and economic decline of the Byzantine Empire naturally formed the backdrop of the lives of ordinary people in Anatolia, Greece and the Balkans, the Crusades in particular were only one aspect of this very complex situation.

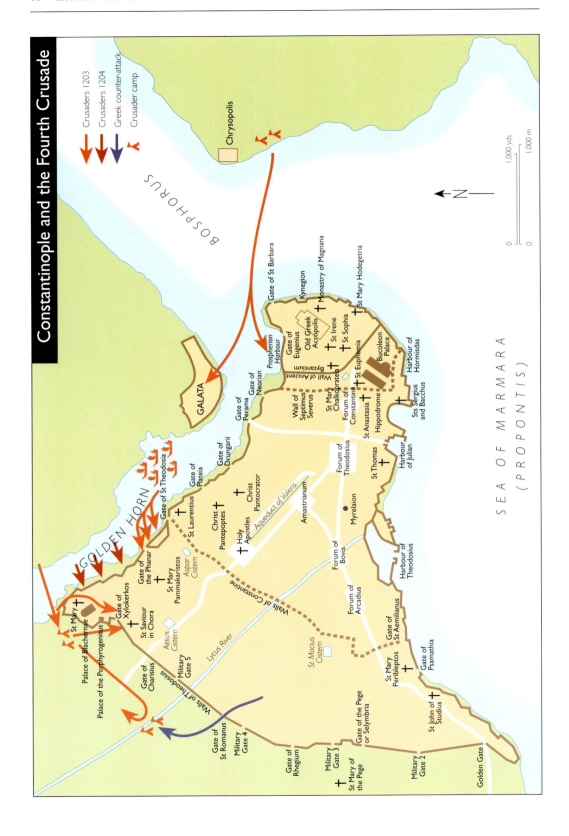

Constantinople and the Fourth Crusade

Crusaders 1203
Crusaders 1204
Greek counter-attack
Crusader camp

BOSPHORUS

Chrysopolis

N

1,000 yds
1,000 m
0
0

Gate of St Barbara
Kynegion
Monastry of Magnana
St Mary Hodegetria
Prospherion Harbour
Gate of Eugenius
Old Greek Acropolis
St Irene
St Sophia
GALATA
Gate of Perama
Gate of Neorian
Wall of Ancient Byzantium
St Mary Chalkoprateia
St Euphemia
Bucoleon Palace
Harbour of Hormisdas
Wall of Septimus Severus
Forum of Constantine
St Anastasia
Hippodrome
Sts Sergius and Bacchus
Gate of Drungarii
Gate of Plateia
Christ Pantocrator
Forum of Theodosius
St Thomas
Harbour of Julian
GOLDEN HORN
Gate of St Theodosia
St Laurentius
Christ Pantepoptes
Holy Apostles
Aqueduct of Valens
Amastrianum
Myrelaion
Forum of Bovis
Harbour of Theodosius
Gate of the Phanar
St Mary Pammakaristos
Aspar Cistern
Walls of Constantine
Lycus River
Forum of Arcadius
St Mary
Gate of Xylokerkos
St Saviour in Chora
Aetios Cistern
Military Gate 5
St Mocius Cistern
Gate of St Aemilianus
Gate of Psamathia
Palace of Blachernae
Palace of the Porphyrogenitus
Gate of Charisius
Walls of Theodosius
St Mary Peribleptos
St John of Studius
Gate of St Romanus
Military Gate 4
Gate of Rhegium
Military Gate 3
St Mary of the Pege
Gate of the Pege or Selymbria
Military Gate 2
Golden Gate

SEA OF MARMARA
(PROPONTIS)

The advice given by one of Saladin's senior amirs before the Hattin campaign, according to Ibn al-Athir:

"I advise that we cross their territory, pillaging, devastating, burning and taking captives. And if a Frankish army faces us, we fight them. Certainly the people of the east (eastern Islamic territory) criticise us and complain, saying that Saladin has given up the jihad and prefers to attack fellow Muslims."

Much the same could be said of the impact the Crusades had on the lives of ordinary people in the Islamic world, whether they were Muslims, Christians or Jews. The political and cultural elite of those regions actually conquered by the Crusaders, and which became the Crusader States, were largely wiped out, driven out or fled. Those who remained were by and large the rural peasantry and some nomadic Bedouin tribes of the semi-desert frontier. The former merely exchanged masters, though they also lost their culturally important educated leadership. For the latter the change of 'masters' was more apparent than real. They had largely kept themselves at a distance from the previous Islamic governments and now kept themselves similarly distant from the Crusader conquerors. Elsewhere in the Islamic world the impact of the Crusades on ordinary people was either very localised, as in Anatolia, Syria and Egypt, or was so distant as to be little more than a source of stories.

One of the most lasting impacts the Crusades had upon the Islamic lands of the Middle East was to stimulate bigotry against local or indigenous Christian communities. Whether this rising tide of intolerance,

The caravanserai or khan at Agzi Kara Han on the Aksaray-Kayseri road in central Anatolia was one of many such 'medieval motels' built during the Seljuk period. Each had sufficiently strong fortifications to deter bandits or highway robbers but not of course real armies. Meanwhile those which were royal foundations such as Agzi Kara Han, begun in 1231, had splendidly decorated entrance portals which declared the power of the Seljuk ruler who built them. (David Nicolle photograph)

Travellers or pilgrims in a manuscript made in Baghdad in 1237. Here the artist, Yahya Ibn Mahmud al-Wasiti, shows four travellers, all in distinctive costumes indicating their ages and perhaps professions. One of the younger men at the front rides a mule rather than a horse; the animal having a perhaps decorative horse-blanket made from animal skins. (*Maqamat of al-Hariri*, Ms. Arabe 5847, f.117, Bibliothèque Nationale, Paris, France)

which the Crusades were in part intended to 'save' nothing less than a disaster.

Following the First Crusade and the establishment of the Crusader States in Syria-Palestine, the legitimacy of Crusader conquests became a matter of great concern to several legal scholars during this period. The clash between the basic pacifism of Christianity and the reality of warfare had been a concern for theologians and lawyers alike for many centuries. This then became even more of a problem with the development of ideas of 'Holy War' against non-Christians and the enemies of the Church. As a consequence churchmen and scholars laid increasing emphasis on texts drawn from the Judaic Old Testament rather than the Christian New Testament, since war was less of a problem in the former. Meanwhile the parallels between Christian Holy War and Islamic Jihad were probably not a result of direct influence in one direction or the other, but may have resulted from similar responses to similar ethical and political problems: both drawing upon

so unlike the cultural co-existence of the preceding Golden Age of Islamic civilisation from the 7th to the 11th centuries, was inevitable or was a direct result of the Crusades is unclear. What is clear is that Christians had been in a majority in Anatolia, Egypt, much of Syria and perhaps even parts of Iraq, and had been flourishing minorities in several other territories at the moment when the First Crusaders burst upon the scene. By the time the Crusader city of Acre fell in 1291 they were minorities almost everywhere, increasingly suspect to their Muslim rulers and neighbours alike. The fact that the status, role and even the size of Jewish communities did not suffer a similar collapse may perhaps be taken as evidence that the Crusades were, from the point of view of those Eastern Christian communities

From a letter by an elderly Jewish pilgrim from North Africa or Andalus, written in Alexandria and expressing his hope that the Fatimid Caliph will retake Jerusalem and thus enable the writer to visit the Holy City:

"Now all of us had anticipated that our Sultan [the Caliph], may God bestow glory upon his victories, would set out against them with his troops and chase them away. But time after time our hope failed. Yet to this very moment we hope that God will give his enemies into his hands, for it is inevitable that the armies will join in battle this year. If God grants us victory through him and he conquers Jerusalem ... I shall not be amongst those who linger but shall go there to behold the city, and shall afterwards return straight to you, if God wills it ... because at my age I cannot afford to wait any longer."

Poetic verses by al-'Umarah from his lamentations for the murder of the Fatimid Caliph al-Zafir and his two brothers in 1149, with praise for the wazir al-Tala'i who restored order:

"How sadly I sigh for descendants of the Prophet who were more than rainfall for humanity and food for the sorrowful. Their entrails are now scattered in every mountain pass, their bodies have been cut down everywhere ... Radiance is yours, about which the Koran, the Torah and the Gospels all sing words of praise ... Our spirit decided to describe such lives in verses, with you as their subject, while the Archangel Gabriel took care of the prose. These are characteristics which you imposed upon the religion of Muhammad, which Salih al-Tala'i [Salih 'the Just Leader'] stoutly defended. Sufficient is he; he is the door, and only through him can You [God] be reached."

earlier Judaic and other ideas. Although the only real pacifists in medieval Europe were Cathars or Albigensians and other 'heretics', criticism of both Crusaders and Crusading grew. At first it seemed to be limited to criticism of the resident aristocracy of the Crusader States in the Middle East and Greece who were often regarded as too willing to make a political accommodation with their Muslim neighbours and supposed enemies, as insufficiently dedicated to the ideal of Holy War and as having gone soft as a result of adopting local Middle East or Islamic ways of life. Meanwhile the

The Crucifixion in a Jacobite Gospel from the Jazira region of north-eastern Syria, south-eastern Turkey and northern Iraq, made between 1216 and 1220. The closest artistic parallels to this Eastern Christian style of manuscript illustration is found in Islamic painting from the same regions rather than with Byzantine or Western European art. The same is largely true of the arms and armour of military figures such as the soldiers dividing Christ's cloak or the Centurion on the far right. (Ms. Add. 7170, f.151r; British Library, London, England)

The Mausoleum of Esther and Mordechai, next to the synagogue in Hamadan, Iran, largely dates from the central medieval period, though its massive granite door probably survives from an earlier structure. The walls have inscriptions in Hebrew, Aramaic and Arabic while the tombs are carved from ebony covered with cloth veils. According to tradition Esther and her uncle Mordechai interceded with the ancient Persian Emperor Xerxes on behalf of her oppressed people. In fact the tombs are more likely to cover the grave of the Jewish wife of the Sassanian king Yezdegird (399-421). During the subsequent medieval period there were flourishing Jewish communities throughout most Islamic countries, including that at Hamadan. They played a major cultural and economic role, but sometimes also rose to political importance. (David Nicolle photograph)

popularity and reputation of the Military Orders generally remained high, even when criticism of the Church as a whole increased in the later 13th century. In fact, many Western European Christians regarded the Military Orders as the best part of the Church. Nevertheless, there was a growing feeling that the Templars were too fond of money and the Hospitallers too fond of their horses, while the fall of Acre in 1291 brought widespread criticism of the Templars, though less of the Hospitallers.

There was similarly something of a paradox in the way Western Christendom came to view Islam and the Islamic world during the Crusading era. On the one hand ignorance and fear, mingled with admiration for an undoubtedly more sophisticated civilisation seen in the early medieval period, was replaced by greater knowledge and even a degree of understanding among a part of the Western cultural elite. The anti-Islamic horror story propaganda, which had been widely believed at the time of the First Crusade and immediately afterwards, declined while antipathy towards the Byzantines and other Orthodox Christians increased. Christian scholars wrote careful refutations of Islamic belief, based upon a more accurate knowledge of their subject. During the 13th century there was growing interest in the

possibility of the conversion of Muslims rather than merely the destruction of Islam by military means. These changes naturally led to the study of Arabic and other oriental languages. A few scholars, recognising a considerable overlap in the beliefs of Christians and Muslims, even started to portray Muslims as heretics rather than pagans. These new attitudes were summed up by the scholar Ricoldus around 1294, who wrote of Muslims: 'We have been amazed that amongst the followers of so perfidious a law, works of so great perfection are found.' Nevertheless, this remained a minority view.

The 12th and 13th centuries saw some of the most significant movements of peoples during the Middle Ages, although not on the scale of the Age of Migrations, which accompanied the fall of the Roman Empire. Nor did they have such a wide-ranging cultural and political impact as the Arab-Islamic expansion of the 7th–8th centuries.

Men and women watch a physician preparing medicines, in a manuscript made in northern Iraq at the end of the 12th century. Islamic medicine and surgery techniques were, of course, far in advance of those of Christian Western Europe. This manuscript also includes numerous views of everyday life, such as the women's and children's costumes, the half starved beggar and the special form of oven seen here. (*Kitab al-Diryaq*, Ms. Arabe 2964, f.15, Bibliothèque Nationale, Paris, France)

The population movements and migrations of the Crusading era were more localised but just as dramatic. However, very few of them were a direct result of the Crusades themselves. The Turkish conquest, repopulation and linguistic absorption of previously Byzantine Anatolia was neither caused nor halted by the Crusades, though it was certainly slowed down by them. Similarly the large-scale Armenian migration from eastern Anatolia to Cilicia in the south was not caused by the Crusades, but by previous events along the eastern frontier of the Byzantine Empire. Population movements seen within the Byzantine and non-Byzantine Balkans also had very little to do with the Crusades. The Christian so-called Reconquista of the Iberian peninsula from the Muslims of Andalusia was closely related to the Crusading movement, but nevertheless remained a separate series of events. The northern Italian colonisation and indeed 'Italianisation' of parts of southern Italy and the great island of Sicily which followed the Norman conquest of these regions was similarly a separate though parallel event to the Crusades. To a large extent the Arabisation of previously Berber North Africa was a phenomenon of the 11th to 14th centuries rather than of the Arab-Islamic conquest

The ruins of the huge Ayn Diwar bridge still stand next to the River Tigris in Syria, within sight of the Turkish frontier and only a few kilometres from the Iraqi border. It was constructed in the 12th or early 13th century and its vast central arch still stands witness to the skill of medieval Islamic architecture, as well as to the importance which local rulers gave to commercial and military communications. (David Nicolle photograph)

four centuries earlier, but again it had nothing to do with the Crusades. Clearly, the astonishing Turkish and subsequently Mongol expansion out of Central Asia, which was one of the most important population and cultural movements of this period, owed nothing to the Crusades. The number of Western Europeans who settled within the Crusader States in both the Middle East and Greece remained quite small, and although they had a profound cultural and linguistic impact on several areas in the 12th and 13th centuries, the changes they brought about were rolled back and almost entirely eradicated as the Crusader States themselves collapsed.

In terms of population movements and migrations, the Crusades themselves had a dramatic but localised and temporary effect. They remained a colourful and adventurous – perhaps even heroic – episode for all the peoples involved, but their lasting impact was minimal.

A saint, a lady, a scholar and a rabbi

Saint or Sufi?

Francis of Assisi was born in 1182, the son of Pietro Bernardone, a prosperous cloth merchant, and he spent his youth in pleasure and extravagance. In Italy, however, the wealthy middle class also defended their cities as cavalry and so Francis fought against Perugia in 1201. Francis joined another military expedition around 1205 but was halted by a religious dream on the road. As a result he renounced the sword in favour of living as a hermit and caring for the poor. Francis did not, however, give up writing verses in the style of the troubadours, though his subjects were now religious. They also strongly resembled those of a great Islamic mystic or Sufi, Jalal al-Din Rumi, who lived many years in Anatolia and was alive during Francis' lifetime.

There were, in fact, an extraordinary number of similarities between Francis of Assisi's writings, teaching and way of life and those of some contemporary Islamic mystical teachers. Islamic scholars note these with pride though Christian historians tend to ignore them. Francis was about 30 years old when he first headed for Syria but turned back through lack of money. Later he tried again through Spain and Morocco but was unsuccessful. Next Francis followed the Fifth Crusaders to Egypt, where he went to see Sultan al-Kamil and was well received. Some Muslim scholars suggest that Francis' journeys were an effort to find the Arab roots of the medieval minstrel tradition and perhaps of Sufi ideas.

Even Francis' famous association with animals has parallels in the life of Najm al-Din Kubra, founder of a Sufi order known as the 'Greater Brothers' which had many followers in the Middle East when Francis visited the area. After returning from Egypt, Francis wrote his First Rule, for followers who would in time develop into the Order of Franciscan Friars Minor or 'Lesser Brothers'. The Franciscans' habitual salutation of 'The peace of God be with you' is, of course, a direct translation of the Arabic 'Salam alaykum'.

The lady of Beirut

Isabella was a great-granddaughter of John of Ibelin, the lord of Beirut. She succeeded to this *fief* on the death of her father and was married as a child to King Hugh II of Cyprus. Hugh soon died, after which Isabella had two further husbands. Meanwhile she faced a new and aggressive neighbour, Sultan Baybars of Egypt and Syria, although he was more lenient to Isabella than to other Crusader rulers.

At one time Isabella of Beirut had been a 'virgin widow' but soon lost this reputation. In fact her affair with Julian of Sidon led to papal condemnation. Nevertheless, a treaty between Beirut and the Mamluk Sultan in 1269 described Isabella as 'the exalted, virtuous and glorious queen … the lady of Beirut'. In 1272 she married the English knight Hamo l'Estrange, who may have been one of Prince Edward of England's companions. Next year, on his deathbed, Hamo placed Beirut under the protection of Baybars, but King Hugh III of Cyprus-Jerusalem hoped to use the eligible heiress Isabella to attract another powerful baron to the east. He forcibly took Isabella to Cyprus to arrange another marriage. Baybars objected strongly, the King gave way and Isabella returned to Beirut, where Baybars provided her with a mamluk guard. Isabella remained in her beloved Beirut until her death around 1282.

From a letter by the great Jewish scholar Maimonides to Samuel Ibn Judah Ibn Tibbon, translator of his Guide for the Perplexed:

"My duties to the Sultan are very heavy. I am obliged to visit him every day, early in the morning and when he or any of his children or any of the women in his *harim* are unwell … It also frequently happens that one or two of his royal officers fall sick, and I must attend to their healing. So, as a rule, I go to al-Qahira (the royal quarter of Cairo, quite a long way from Maimonides' house) very early in the day, and even if nothing unusual happens I do not return until the afternoon, by which time I am almost dying of hunger … I dismount from my animal, wash my hands, go to the patients (who are waiting in the antechambers of his house) and beg them to be patient while I eat a light meal, the only meal I have in twenty-four hours … When night falls I am so exhausted that I can scarcely speak."

A guide for sultans and pilgrims

Shaykh Taqi al-Din Abu'l-Hasan 'Ali Ibn Abu Bakr al-Harawi al-Mawsili was born in Mosul, though his family came from Afghanistan. He became a preacher in Baghdad and Aleppo. As an ascetic and writer al-Harawi spent much of his life on pilgrimages to sacred sites. His last years were spent in Aleppo, where the local Ayyubid prince built him a *madrasa* or teaching mosque near one of the city gates. Popularly known as 'the wandering ascetic', al-Harawi's writings indicate a huge spread of interests and an enquiring mind. They include a guide to Islamic pilgrimage sites in Palestine, this being an example of the *fada'il* or praise literature designed to increase the importance of Crusader-occupied territories in Islamic eyes.

Many of al-Harawi's journeys seem to have been intelligence-gathering or

diplomatic missions, extending beyond Syria and Palestine to Egypt, Anatolia and Sicily between 1173 and 1189. He also accompanied Saladin on military expeditions and his book *The Ruses of War* and his *Political Testament* show a thorough grasp of the realities of Crusading warfare and diplomacy. Al-Harawi died in 1215 and was buried in his teaching mosque in Aleppo.

The greatest rabbi

Moses Ben Maimon, better known as Maimonides, was born in 1135 in Cordoba. He is regarded as the greatest figure in medieval Judaism. The family had to leave Andalus because of increasing religious intolerance following the al-Muwahhid conquest in 1148. For many years they travelled around North Africa. All except Maimonides converted to Islam in the 1150s. Maimonides himself continued his studies, including medicine, and also began to write. In 1165 the Maimon family sailed to Crusader Acre but finally they settled down in Egypt, where the atmosphere was more tolerant. Following his father's death, Maimonides played a leading role in the flourishing Egyptian Jewish community and described his next eight years as being free from care.

Partly supported by his brother David, a jewel merchant, Maimonides dedicated himself to scholarship and his duties as a religious leader. But in 1169 David drowned while on a trading expedition across the Indian Ocean, leaving the family destitute. Maimonides was now in charge and, after a

Assisi as seen from the Rocca Maggiore castle, looking towards the green dome of the mid-13th century Church of Santa Chiara, which contains several relics of St Francis of Assisi. This was the saint's home town and, like most Italian cities of the period, it was dominated as much by the wealthy merchant middle class as by the aristocracy and the Church. Here the future founder of the Order of Franciscan Friars grew up in a privileged, prosperous but not aristocratic environment, learning to play and compose the troubadour verses which would later be reflected in his religious writings. (David Nicolle photograph)

year of psychological collapse, he decided to earn his living as a doctor. By 1185 his reputation was so high that he became a personal physician to Saladin's wazir, al-Fadl. According to legend Maimonides was even consulted by Richard the Lionheart. Following the death of his first wife, Maimonides married the sister of one of the sultan's secretaries. He was now a famous man who, as a leader of his community, corresponded with other Jewish communities across most of the known world. His greatest works were the *Mishnah Torah* and the *Guide for the Perplexed*. Maimonides died in 1204 and his body was taken to Tiberius, where his grave still exists.

The rise of the Mamluks and the fall of the Crusader State

By the second half of the 13th century the Crusader States in Syria and Palestine had been reduced to a series of separate coastal enclaves. None had much of a hinterland and all were to a greater or lesser extent dominated by coastal hills or mountains that were now firmly under Islamic control. Meanwhile enthusiasm for the Crusading movement had slumped in Western Europe. Help from this direction for the remnants of the Crusader States was intermittent, inadequate and generally unpredictable. To the east the Mongol threat to Syria had been contained if not yet entirely removed by the Mamluk Sultans and their astonishingly efficient army. However, the remaining Crusader-held coastal enclaves included several wealthy and very strongly fortified cities plus a handful of mighty castles. Both sides recognised that these would be hard nuts to crack.

From the Mamluk-Islamic point of view the Crusader outposts remained a strategic threat. They could not only serve as bridgeheads for future Crusades but such Crusades might also establish a genuine alliance with the more immediately dangerous Mongols, or Il-Khans as they were soon known. At the same time there must have been a widespread desire in Syria, Egypt and other parts of the Islamic Middle East to 'finish the job' by completing a task of reconquest started by Imad al-Din Zangi and Nur al-Din, Saladin, Baybars and others. Indeed the Islamic liberation of the remaining Crusader outposts had acquired a certain momentum and inevitability of its own. This certainly appeared to be the case once the major political, military and economic powers of Western Europe were no longer so interested in the survival of places such as Acre.

Following the Mamluk defeat of the Mongols at the battle of 'Ayn Jalut in 1260, the final phase of the major Crusading Wars in the Middle East consisted of a series of sieges. This, of course, excludes those naval or raiding expeditions of the 14th century that were graced with the title of Crusade. Some of these last sieges were of massive proportions and culminated in the fall of Acre itself in 1291. The coastal cities of Caesarea and Arsuf fell to the Mamluks in 1265. Safad, the last major inland town held by the Crusaders, fell the following year, followed by Jaffa and Antioch in 1268.

The 1270s saw a respite for the surviving Crusader enclaves, though Prince Edward of England's so-called 'Little' Crusade in 1271 hardly strengthened what remained. Nevertheless, a ten-year truce was agreed between the Kingdom of Jerusalem and the Mamluk Sultanate the following year. This enabled the great Sultan Baybars to direct the final campaigns of his life against the Christian Kingdom of Cilician Armenia, a vassal of the Mongol Il-Khans, and against the Il-Khans themselves in northern Syria.

Although the Mamluks' epic struggle against the Mongol invaders continued through the 1280s and beyond, Sultan Qalawun still found the time and troops to take the huge Hospitaller castle of Margat in 1285. Four years later he overwhelmed Tripoli and to all intents and purposes brought the County of Tripoli to an end. Meanwhile the supposedly united Crusader Kingdoms of Jerusalem and Cyprus were rent by internal dissention and civil conflict.

The death of the warlike Sultan Qalawun in 1290 did not bring any respite, for in 1291 his son and heir, Sultan al-Ashraf Khalil, rejected a desperate plea for peace from Acre and prepared for the final showdown. As this last siege loomed, help at

The inner citadel and inner moat of Krak des Chevaliers castle. Krak was the strongest or at least most impressive of the fortifications held by the Order of Hospitallers during the last decades of the Crusader States in the Middle East. Nevertheless, it fell to the Mamluks after a siege of little more than a month in 1271. The section shown here dates from the second phase of construction from the late 12th century to its capture by the Mamluks. It faces south, over the moat, narrow outer ward and relatively low outer wall towards the only direction from which an attacker could realistically approach. As such this sloping glacis, wall and towers formed the strongest part of the entire defensive system. (David Nicolle photograph)

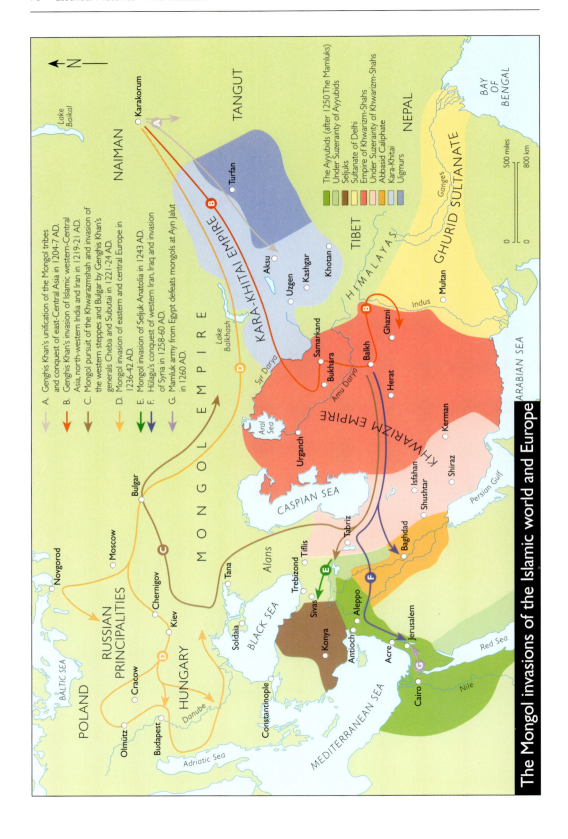

A. Genghis Khan's unification of the Mongol tribes and conquest of east-Central Asia in 1204-7 AD.
B. Genghis Khan's invasion of Islamic western-Central Asia, north-western India and Iran in 1219-21 AD.
C. Mongol pursuit of the Khwarazmshah and invasion of the western steppes and Bulgar by Genghis Khan's generals Cheba and Subutai in 1221-24 AD.
D. Mongol invasion of eastern and central Europe in 1236-42 AD.
E. Mongol invasion of Seljuk Anatolia in 1243 AD.
F. Hülagu's conquest of western Iran, Iraq and invasion of Syria in 1258-60 AD.
G. Mamluk army from Egypt defeats mongols at Ayn Jalut in 1260 AD.

The Mongol invasions of the Islamic world and Europe

Crusader Acre and the Mamluk siege of AD 1291

1. Army of Hamah (and other northern Syrian vassal contingents).
2. Army of Damascus (Mamluk).
3. Army of Egypt (Mamluk).
4. Tent and HQ of Mamluk Sultan al-Ashraf Khalil.
5. Christian ships bombard the flanks of the Mamluk siege lines.
6. Templars.
7. Hospitallers.
8. Army of the Kingdom of Cyprus and Jerusalem.
9. Teutonic Knights.
10. French.
11. English.
12. Pisans.
13. Genoese.
A. Templars' sortie from Porte St Lazare during night of 15-16 April against the Ayyubid
   contingent from Hamah fails to destroy the Mamluk mangonels.
B. Second nighttime sortie from Porte St. Antione by Hospitallers driven back with loss.
C. Arrival of King Henry II of Cyprus and Jerusalem with reinforcements on 4 May.
D. Main Mamluk mining operations directed towards the New Tower; section of wall collapses
   on 15 May; Mamluks take New Tower on 16 May and prepare to attack a breach in the inner wall near Porte St. Antoine.
E. Mamluk army launches general assault on the walls from the Porte St. Antoine to the Patriarch's Tower at dawn, 18 May.
F. One Mamluk column scales a breach in the inner wall near the Tower Maudite before sunrise 18 May,
   then extends along the wall towards the Porte St. Antoine.
G. Mamluks break through into the city around 3.00pm of 18 May.
H. French and English, including Othon de Grandson, escape to the harbour and thence to Cyprus.
I. Fugitives including King Henry II of Cyprus and Jerusalem escape from the Templar Castle to Cyprus.
J. Last stand of the Templars in the Templar Castle until 28 May when they are overrun and virtually exterminated.

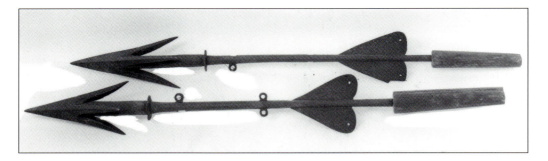

The staves or bows of two large crossbows and two massive iron arrows which might have been shot from such siege-crossbows. They were found in the Citadel of Damascus in the early 20th century and probably date from the 13th or 14th centuries. One of the bows is of normal composite construction, though larger than an ordinary hand-bow. The other is regularly curved, has a rectangular section and is very similar to some other Middle Eastern Islamic crossbow staves whose internal structure, though composite, is very different to that of the ordinary Islamic composite bow. (invs. L1, L2 & L3, Musée de l'Armée, Paris, France)

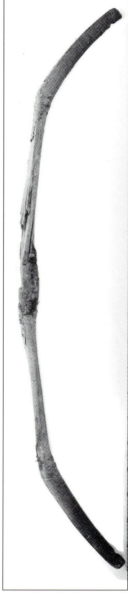

last arrived from Western Europe but once again it was fragmentary, unco-ordinated and insufficient. As a result Acre fell on 18 May 1291. The remaining fragments of Crusader territory to the north and south either were abandoned or accepted Mamluk domination over the next few months.

A Templar garrison did, however, hold out on the Syrian offshore island of Ruad. Attempts were even made to use this tiny, rocky islet with its small castle and exposed harbours just a few hundred metres from the Syrian coast as a base from which to launch counter-attacks. They failed and in 1302 Ruad was overwhelmed. Now all that remained of the Crusader invasion of the Middle East in the late 1090s were the Kingdom of Cyprus and what was in many ways the 'Crusader' Kingdom of Cilician Armenia. Both would endure for many more years; the rump of Cilician Armenia finally falling to a Mamluk assault in 1375. Meanwhile the Mamluk Sultan al-Nasir had defeated the last major Mongol invasion of Syria at Marj al-Suffar in 1303. The Kingdom of Cyprus eventually passed into Venetian hands before falling to the Ottoman Turks in the 16th century.

The failure of an idea and the rebirth of Islamic expansionism

As in almost all medieval wars, the casualties and material damage caused by the Crusades were relatively light and generally localised. More people died of disease or starvation as a direct or indirect result of these campaigns than were killed in battles or sieges. However, the losses incurred by the losing side in a major battle or prolonged siege could be huge in relation to the numbers of people actually involved. During and immediately after the First Crusade the Christians showed a degree of fanaticism and ferocity that shocked their Muslim opponents, since the latter had been used to the relatively restrained and almost gentlemanly inter-Islamic or Islamic-Byzantine conflicts of previous decades. This Crusader ferocity sometimes reappeared in later campaigns but generally speaking the invaders gradually came to recognise that their Muslim opponents were men much like themselves, though of course 'misguided'. For their part Islamic armies rarely indulged in the large-scale slaughter characteristic of the early Crusaders and, of course, of the Mongol invasions of the 13th century. The occasional ruthlessness of Islamic leaders or armies was usually undertaken in a controlled manner for a specific or immediate purpose. One such example was Saladin's execution of captured Templars and Hospitallers after his victory at Hattin.

Another particularly interesting aspect of Crusading warfare was the way in which the Crusaders changed their attitude towards the possibility of being taken prisoner. At the time of the First Crusade the Crusaders, unlike their fellow Christians who were fighting the Islamic Moors in Spain, seem not to have considered being taken alive by the enemy. For some time afterwards there was no apparent system for the ransoming or exchange of prisoners. As the years passed, however, these Westerners clearly learned from the long-established prisoner exchange and ransom system which had made earlier conflicts between Orthodox Christian Byzantine and Islamic armies more tolerable. Even when such systems were established captives could remain in prison or serve as slaves for a very long time – sometimes for the rest of their lives.

Many captured Crusaders, including knights as well as ordinary soldiers and even occasionally members of the elite Military Orders, abandoned all hope of returning home. As a consequence some converted to Islam and entered the service of their captors. This was particularly apparent during the second half of the 13th century and some of these ex-prisoners rose to positions of military authority in the Mamluk army. The same had happened in the opposite direction when the Crusaders

The cost of war materials and shipping for the Crusade of 1252, as recorded in the Royal Accounts of King Louis IX:

"The pay of knights serving for wages – £57,093. 17s. 10d; Gifts and subsidies promised to knights serving without wages – £23,253. 18s. 4d; Wages of mounted crossbowmen and sergeants – £22,242. 13s. 6d; Replacement of 264 war-horses – £6,789. 17s; Wages of infantry crossbowmen and sergeants – £29,575. 0s. 6d; Wages of carpenters, siege engineers and labourers – £689, 12s. 3d; Pay for labourers in towns overseas – £41,366. 14s. 9d; Cost of ransoming captives – £967. 13s. 9d; Other miscellaneous expenditure – £24,429. 11s; Costs of shipping – £5,725. 15s. Total – £212,164. 13. 11d.

The Mamluk Sultanate c. AD 1295 and the end of the Crusader States

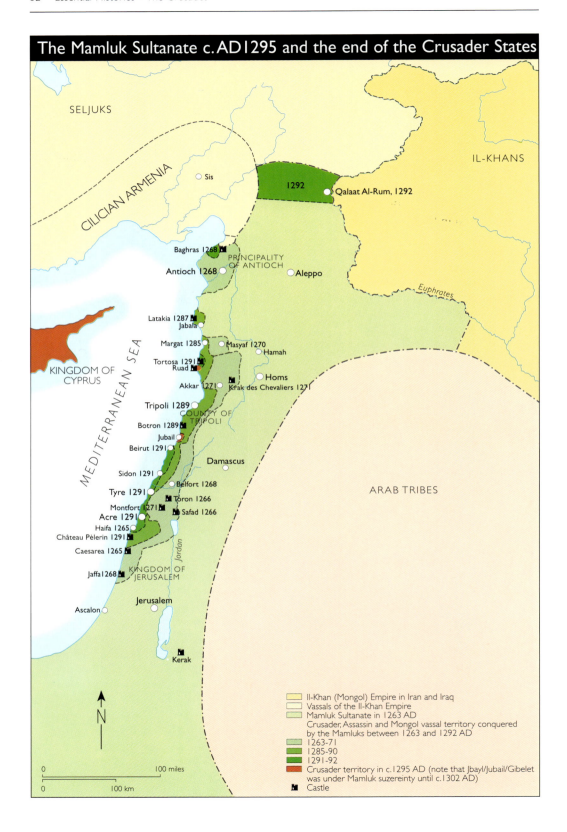

SELJUKS

IL-KHANS

CILICIAN ARMENIA

Sis

1292

Qalaat Al-Rum, 1292

Baghras 1268
PRINCIPALITY OF ANTIOCH
Antioch 1268
Aleppo

Euphrates

Latakia 1287
Jabala
Margat 1285
Masyaf 1270
Hamah
Tortosa 1291
Ruad
Akkar 1271
Krak des Chevaliers 1271
Homs

MEDITERRANEAN SEA

KINGDOM OF CYPRUS

Tripoli 1289
COUNTY OF TRIPOLI
Botron 1289
Jubail
Beirut 1291
Damascus
Sidon 1291
Belfort 1268
Tyre 1291
Toron 1266
Montfort 1271
Safad 1266
Acre 1291
Haifa 1265
Château Pèlerin 1291
Caesarea 1265
Jordan
Jaffa 1268
KINGDOM OF JERUSALEM
Jerusalem
Ascalon

ARAB TRIBES

Kerak

N

0   100 miles
0   100 km

Il-Khan (Mongol) Empire in Iran and Iraq
Vassals of the Il-Khan Empire
Mamluk Sultanate in 1263 AD
Crusader, Assassin and Mongol vassal territory conquered by the Mamluks between 1263 and 1292 AD
1263-71
1285-90
1291-92
Crusader territory in c.1295 AD (note that Jbayl/Jubail/Gibelet was under Mamluk suzereinty until c.1302 AD)
Castle

After the Muslims retook Jerusalem from the Crusaders for the last
time they started a building programme in the Holy City on the Haram
al-Sharif or Temple Mount. Here, in the north-western corner of the
Haram al-Sharif, the minaret of the Ghawanimah Madrasah or religious
college was erected in 1297, then restored in AD 1329. A mosque and
minaret were also built facing the Christian Church of the Holy
Sepulchre. The indigenous Christians and visiting Christian pilgrims were
largely left in peace, but such buildings confirmed who was now in
charge. (David Nicolle photograph)

captured many Muslim prisoners in the 12th century. Some of these men became the famous turcopoles, who were equipped as light cavalry and operated in traditional Middle Eastern style in Byzantine or Crusader service. In both cases such apostates were normally executed if recaptured by their previous colleagues. It also seems to have been true that, when captured, soldiers were more likely to be executed than civilians, the old more likely than the young, and senior men rather than ordinary troops unless they were considered worth a ransom. On all sides the treatment of prisoners tended to be milder when the captors were enjoying a period of success, and harsher when the captors were enduring a period of defeat.

The fact that Muslims so clearly won the wars of the Crusades in the Middle East caused a deep wound to Christian Western European self-esteem. The success of Christian arms against the Muslims in Spain and Portugal could not somehow balance the loss of the Holy Land. Even the Ottoman Turkish conquest and domination of so much of south-eastern Europe did not seem to be such a psychological hurt. Of course the Ottoman Empire eventually crumbled and collapsed, whereas the defeat of the Crusaders in Palestine continued to rankle right up to modern times. Perhaps as a result the British capture of Jerusalem during the First World War was presented as a sort of Crusade, or as the final overturning of

Islamic victories in the 12th and 13th centuries. Similarly the terms 'Crusade' and 'Crusader' have become synonymous with struggles against evil, both personal and political, in several European languages. Sadly the corresponding Arab-Islamic terms Jihad and *Mujahid* seem well on the way to becoming terms of abuse in the Western political and cultural vocabulary. In fact the Crusades continue to hang like a dark cloud over relations between the Christian or so-called Western world and the world of Islam.

On the Islamic side, the defeat of the Crusades naturally boosted cultural, political and military self-confidence. This confidence was further enhanced by the Ottoman Turks when they carried the conflict deep inside Christian territory over the next few centuries. However, the struggle against the Crusaders and the Mongols resulted in a form of fundamental cultural retrenchment within Islam's Middle Eastern heartland. Political and cultural conservatism now dominated and although there was progress in some fields, the Islamic world gradually fell behind Europe in economic, military, scientific, political and to some extent even artistic terms.

This religiously based conservatism was epitomised in the role and writings of Ibn Taimiyah, who lived in the early Mamluk Sultanate. Ibn Taimiyah was a legal and religious scholar, deeply concerned with the prolonged war between the Mamluks and the superficially Muslim Il-Khan Mongols of later 13th- and early 14th-century Iran. The relative unimportance of the Crusades by that time is illustrated by the fact that Ibn Taimiyah barely gave them a mention. Though concerned about the role and status of non-Muslims in Islamic states, Ibn Taimiyah was particularly emphatic about the need for Sunni Islamic political dominance and he was very anti-Shi'a. He also saw the Mongol conqueror Genghis Khan's *Yasa* or legal code as a form of 'rational law and political system'. As such it was a genuine rival to divinely inspired Islamic *Shari'a* law. His awareness of the cultural problem may have reflected Ibn

Saladin's supposed orders or speech before the siege of Tyre in 1187, according to 'Imad al-Din al-Isfahani:
"Improve and complete the siege engines, bring up and push forward the mangonels, prepare and assemble the bastions and movable towers, advance and align the palisades and bulwarks, flatten and level the emplacements ready for mangonels, relieve the army of its cumbersome baggage, prepare the stones and pots of *naft* ..."

The effigy of Conrad Werner de Haltstatt, who died in 1283, is one of the most neglected sources in the study of Western European armour at a time when Islamic and perhaps Mongol influence had stimulated the development of early forms of semi-rigid body protection. The apparently unique system of loops and a sliding bolt or turn buckle is only shown on the Alsacian knight's right shoulder. It secures a *coat-of-plates* which is worn over an ordinary mail hauberk. The carving itself came from the Unterlinden Convent and is otherwise very similar to many other late 13th-century effigies from what was then the German Empire. (Unterlinden Museum, Colmar, France. David Nicolle photograph)

Taimiyah's famous ability to see both sides of an argument, but it did not stop his outright condemnation of those he saw as the enemies of Islam. Today Ibn Taimiyah is still a very influential religious thinker and his writings are still widely used by so-called Islamic 'fundamentalists'.

In cultural terms the Crusades were important for a number of reasons. As far as Western Europe was concerned they coincided with the 12th-century Renaissance. Here the arts, sciences and cultural wealth of Islamic civilisation clearly had a major impact on the brilliant cultural revival within Western Europe. Nevertheless, the specific role of the Crusades in this remarkable event is very hard to ascertain. They provided Western European writers, musicians and artists with material for epic poetry, troubadour songs, manuscript illuminations, wall-paintings and a whole array of minor arts. Religious relics and assorted exotic luxury goods were brought back from the Middle East, sometimes as booty, sometimes legitimately purchased. Though few in number, their influence can be seen in a wide variety of artistic forms including abstract decoration and pseudo-Arabic inscriptions in medieval manuscripts, ceramics, textiles and so on. New ideas about architecture and architectural decoration similarly filtered westward. Among other

A fragment of a painted ceramic plate from Egypt or Syria provides some very rare pictorial evidence that some Muslim cavalrymen adopted some features of Western European knightly equipment, such as that used by their Crusader opponents. This rider's harness, saddle, stirrups and even the decorative cloth streamer fluttering from his stirrup leathers are all typically Islamic 12th or 13th century. On the other hand he almost certainly wears a mail hauberk as far as his knees, and full mail *chausses* around his legs. Written sources confirm that this was occasionally done, usually by using captured Crusader armour, but it very rarely appears in the pictorial sources. (inv. 391, Benaki Museum, Athens, Greece)

A mangonel-sling made of thick rawhide, reinforced with ropes sewn between the layers of leather, is the only known surviving piece of a medieval stone-throwing siege machine. It comes from Syria, Iraq or eastern Turkey and was found together with other pieces of military equipment which have been carbon-dated to the late 12th or 13th century. (Private collection)

things these led to a more extensive use of contrasting light and dark stone on Italian churches.

Further south the close political links which developed between the Norman Kingdom of Sicily and Fatimid Egypt in the 12th century had a consequent influence upon Siculo-Norman government systems, court ceremonial, art and architecture. It is even possible that the Norman rulers of Sicily and southern Italy claimed to be inheriting the Fatimid Caliphate's imperial role when they unsuccessfully invaded North Africa.

Meanwhile the Byzantine world was going through a culturally and artistically inward-looking phase – one of several in the history of the Eastern Roman Empire. As a result, outside influences and foreign motifs are hard to find, though they do exist. Whether this minimal cultural impact had anything to do with the Crusades remains doubtful, however.

The same was to a large extent true in the Islamic world, which had little to learn from Europe in the 12th and 13th centuries. Meanwhile the deepening conservatism of Islamic civilisation made any such adoption of outside ideas very difficult. The only major exception was the astonishing influence of Far Eastern and specifically Chinese culture on the arts and even architecture of the eastern Islamic lands, which were conquered and then ruled by the Mongols. Some of this Far Eastern influence penetrated as far as Egypt, but here the Mamluk Sultanate of the mid-13th to 15th centuries became almost as artistically conservative as the Byzantine Empire. Some Western artistic influence can be seen in ceramics, metalwork and on Christian wall-painting in Syria; rather less in Egypt and rather more in Anatolia.

By and large it would probably be true to say that the cultural impact of the Crusades upon the lands surrounding the Eastern Mediterranean and beyond was minimal, superficial and transitory. The cultural superiority enjoyed by the Islamic World in earlier centuries resulted in most Muslims

continuing to despise Western Europe. This
attitude of mind persisted long after the
original cultural and scientific superiority
had been lost. Of course the Crusader States
disappeared before the greatest cultural
flowering of the European Renaissance in the
14th–15th centuries, and so could not serve
as a channel of influence.

In terms of technology, and specifically
in the exchange of military technology,
the flow of ideas was largely from the
Islamic world to Western Europe. Up to the
11th century almost all the new ideas seen
in European arms, armour and siege
technology had come from Byzantium. In
addition there had been a localised Islamic
influence in the Iberian peninsula and from
Islamic Central Asia, via Russia, to
Scandinavia. There also seems to have been
a significant Islamic influence upon the
design of Mediterranean shipping, though
in transport vessels rather than warships.
During the 12th century there was a large
but as yet generally unrecognised Islamic
technological influence upon many aspects
of Western European weaponry, armour,
siege-machines, pyrotechnics and defensive
architecture.

The only real exceptions to this flow from
east to west appeared in the 13th century.
This time there might have been a small
Western European influence upon the
design of fortifications in the Mamluk
Sultanate, plus some influence on ship
design and certain details of weaponry.

The fall of Acre and the loss of Ruad
did not inevitably mean that the Crusades
were over. Naval warfare and coastal raiding
continued in the Eastern Mediterranean and
there were several Islamic attacks on both
Cyprus and Cilician Armenia. But the idea
of 'liberating' Jerusalem from the Muslims
had become little more than a dream to
inspire writers, propagandists and religious
enthusiasts. There were plans for future
Crusades but very little actually happened.

*Ricoldo of Monte Croce was a Dominican
friar and missionary who lived for some
years in Baghdad when it was ruled by
the Mongol Il-Khans during the late
13th century. He greatly admired the
devout Muslims of the city and its
surrounding areas:*

"Who will not be astounded if he
carefully considers how great is the
interest of these same Muslims in study,
their devotion in prayer, their concern
for the poor, their reverence for the
name of God and the prophets and the
Holy Places, their sobriety in manners,
their hospitality to strangers, their
harmony and love for each other?"

The theatre of operations for future
campaigns now moved westward to the
Aegean and Greece. As the Ottoman
Turks advanced into Europe during the later
14th century the battlefield shifted further
still, into the Balkans and almost to the
heart of Europe itself. These so-called Later
Crusades were, however, a separate story,
different in both kind and purpose since
they were defensive, unlike the essentially
offensive Crusades of the 12th and even
13th centuries.

In fact the war in the Middle East and
Eastern Mediterranean wound down because
Western European political and military
leaders were no longer sufficiently interested.
Meanwhile the Mamluks, as the dominant
Islamic military power in this region, had
completed the task of expelling the
Crusaders from Syria-Palestine. Now they
could concentrate on facing the Il-Khan
Mongols who ruled Iran, Iraq and several
neighbouring regions. When the latter
converted to Islam at the start of the
14th century, the rivalry between Mamluks
and Il-Khans became just another internal
Islamic affair.

Further reading

Ambroise, ed. K. Fenwick, K., *The Third Crusade* (1958).

Benvenisti, M., *The Crusaders in the Holy Land* (1970).

Boase, T.S.R., ed., *The Cilician Kingdom of Armenia* (1978).

Burman, E., *The Assassins, Holy Killers of Islam* (1987).

Cahen, C., *Pre-Ottoman Turkey* (1968).

Edbury, P.W., & J.G. Rowe, *William of Tyre* (1988).

Edbury, P.W., ed., *Crusade and Settlement* (1985).

Ehrenkreutz, A.S., *Saladin* (1972).

Elbeheiry, S., *Les Institutions de l'Egypte au Temps des Ayyubids* (1972).

Elisséeff, N., *Nur al-Din, Un Grand Prince Musulman de Syrie au Temps des Croisades (511–569 H./1118–1174)* (1967).

Erdmann, C., *The Origin of the Idea of the Crusade* (1977).

Gabrieli, F., ed., trans. E.J. Costello, *Arab Historians of the Crusades* (1969).

Glubb. J.B., *The Course of Empire: The Arabs and their Successors* (1965).

Glubb, J.B., *The Lost Centuries: From the Muslim Empires to the Renaissance in Europe* (1967).

Hallam, E., ed., *Chronicles of the Crusades* (1989).

Hodgson, M., *The Order of Assassins* (1955).

Holt, P.M., *The Age of the Crusades: The Near East from the Eleventh Century to 1517* (1986).

Humphreys, R.S., *From Saladin to the Mongols: The Ayyubids in Damascus 1193–1260* (1977).

Irwin, R., *The Middle East in the Middle Ages: The Early Mamluk Sultanate 1250–1382* (1986).

Kedar, B.Z., *Crusade and Mission* (1984).

Kedar, B.Z., ed., *The Horns of Hattin* (1992).

Kennedy, H., *Crusader Castles* (London, 1994).

Lawrence, T.E., ed. D. Pringle, *Crusader Castles* (1988).

Lyons, M.C., & D.E.P. Jackson, *Saladin, The Politics of the Holy War* (1982).

Marshall, C., *Warfare in the Latin East, 1192–1291* (1992).

Marzials, F., *Memoires of the Crusades by Villehardoin & De Joinville* (1908).

Mayer, H.E., trans. J. Gillingham, *The Crusades* (1972).

Müller-Wiener, W., *Castles of the Crusaders* (1966).

Nicolle, D.C., *Arms & Armour of the Crusading Era 1050–1350: Islam, Eastern Europe and Asia* (1999).

Nicolle, D.C., *Arms & Armour of the Crusading Era 1050–1350: Western Europe and the Crusader States* (1999).

Nicolle, D.C., *Medieval Warfare Source Book, Volume 2: Christian Europe and its Neighbours* (1996).

Patton, D., *Badr al-Din Lu'lu', Atabeg of Mosul, 1211–1259* (1991).

Pauphilet, A., & Pognon, E., eds., *Historiens et Chroniqueurs du Moyen Age* (1952).

Powell, J.M., *Anatomy of a Crusade, 1213–1221* (1986).

Prawer, J., *Crusader Institutions* (1980).

Prawer, J., *The Crusaders' Kingdom* (1972).

Pringle, D., *The Red Tower* (1986).

Pritchard, J., *The Latin Kingdom of Jerusalem* (1979).

Pryor, J.H., *Geography, Technology, and War: Studies in the maritime history of the Mediterranean 649–1571* (1988).

Queller, D.E., *The Fourth Crusade* (1978).

Regan, G., *Lionhearts, Saladin and Richard I* (1998).

Riley-Smith, J., ed., *The Atlas of the Crusades* (1991).

Riley-Smith, J., *The Crusades, A Short History* (1987).

Riley-Smith, J., *The Feudal Nobility and the Kingdom of Jerusalem* (1973).

Riley-Smith, J., *The First Crusade and the Idea of Crusading* (1986).

Riley-Smith, J., *What were the Crusades?* (1977).

Riley-Smith, L. & J., *The Crusades, Idea and Reality, 1095–1274* (1981).

Runciman, S., *A History of the Crusades* (3 vols., 1951–54).

Setton, K.M., ed., *A History of the Crusades* (to date 1969—).

Siberry, E., *Criticism of Crusading 1095–1274* (1985).

Smail, R.C., *Crusading Warfare (1097–1193)* (1956).

Smail, R.C., *The Crusaders in Syria and the Holy Land* (1973).

Talbot-Rice, T., *The Seljuks* (1961).

Tibble, S., *Monarchy and Lordship in the Latin Kingdom of Jerusalem* (1989).

Upton-Ward, J.M., ed., *The Rule of the Templars* (1989).

Usamah Ibn-Munqidh, ed. P. Hitti, *Memoires of an Arab-Syrian Gentleman* (1927).

Glossary

'Abbasid: Caliphal dynasty of Sunni Islamic persuasion with its capital normally at Baghdad (750–1262), then in Cairo (1262–1517).

ahdath: urban militia in Islamic cities of the Middle East and Egypt.

agulani: Western European corruption of the Arabic term ghulam (see below), professional soldier of slave-recruited origin.

amirate: small Islamic state ruled by an amir.

Andalus: Arab-Islamic name for that part of the Iberian peninsula under Islamic rulers.

archontes: provincial Byzantine elite in the 13th to 14th centuries.

arrière ban: medieval French term for a general levy of men for military service in both Europe and the Crusader States.

atabeg: governor or ruler of a Middle Eastern Islamic state owing allegiance to the Great Seljuk Sultan, originally an adviser to the reigning prince (literally 'father of the prince').

atlab al-mira: supply train in an Arab-Islamic army.

aventail: mail flap protecting chin and throat.

Ayyubid: dynasty of rulers in Egypt and the Fertile Crescent (*see below*), descended from Saladin (1169–1252 in Egypt; after 1462 in part of south-eastern Turkey).

Banu Numayr: powerful Arab tribe in northern Syria.

battaile: medieval French term for the largest combat or organisational unit in a medieval Western European army.

buckler: small hand-held shield.

Caliphate: titular leader of the Islamic world. Note there were several rival Caliphates in the 12th century.

cantle: rear part of a saddle, raised in a war saddle to support the hips and lower back in combat.

caravan: raid into enemy territory launched from the Crusader States, usually by lightly equipped troops; equivalent of the Western European term 'chevauchée' (*see below*).

chas-chastiaus: form of wooden siege-tower, usually attached to or closely associated with mining or entrenchments.

chausses: armour for the thighs and upper legs, either padded or of mail.

chevauchée: medieval French term for a raid into enemy territory.

coat-of-plates: early form of semi-rigid body armour in 13th-century Europe.

coif: close-fitting hood, made of mail in the context of armour.

connétable: medieval French term for a senior official in a royal or noble household responsible for military discipline and organisation; same as constable.

conrois: small cavalry formation, usually close-packed and armed with lances.

Constantinople: capital of the Byzantine Empire, now called Istanbul.

couched: method of grasping a cavalry lance tightly beneath the right shoulder.

dir': Arabic term for a mail hauberk.

Druze: follower of a Middle Eastern religious belief springing from Islam but now considered outside the Islamic 'umma' or community.

fada'il: literary form in praise of certain religious locations.

Fatimids: Caliphal dynasty of Shi'a Islamic persuasion, founded in North Africa but resident in Egypt during the period of the early Crusades (909–1171).

Fertile Crescent: cultivated and cultivatable zone running from southern Palestine and Jordan through Syria and Lebanon, south-eastern Turkey and Iraq to the Persian Gulf.

fief: piece of land allocated to a person as a source of income, usually to a knight to enable him to equip himself and a certain number of followers as soldiers.

fiefs de soudée: source of income, often allocated to a knight, in which the income derives from a commercial or other financial source rather than from the proceeds of agriculture.

fuller: groove running down a sword-blade providing lightness and strength.

geniza: store for documents of all types in a synagogue, most famously the Cairo geniza.

ghulam: professional Islamic soldier of slave-recruited origin, also called a mamluk (*see below*).

Greek Fire: see naft.

halqa: elite professional household regiment or regiments during the Ayyubid period, subsequently downgraded to non-elite units in the Mamluk period.

hamam: public building containing hot and cold baths plus associated facilities, known in Europe as a 'Turkish bath'.

harim: the private section of an Islamic house reserved for women and for the closest males of the family.

hauberk: form of Western European mail armour to protect the body and part or all of the arms.

Hospitaller: member of the military Order of the Hospital of St John.

husban: short dart-like arrow shot via a piece of grooved wood temporarily held against the side of a bow.

ifranj: Arabic term for Western Europeans; literally 'Franks'.

Il-Khan: Mongol ruling dynasty in Iran and Iraq (AD 1256–1353).

iqta': source of income, often a piece of land, allocated to an individual, often a soldier, to enable him to maintain himself and a specified number of followers, but unlike a Western European fief the iqta' could be taken back by the state at any time.

iwan: Perso-Islamic architectural feature in the form of a large arched recess.

januwiyah: Arabic name for a tall infantry shield with a flattened base; probably meaning 'Genoese', as much military equipment was imported from Genoa.

jawshan: form of flexible body armour, usually of lamellar construction.

jihad: Arab-Islamic term for a struggle against evil, either individual and internal, or external in defence of Islam and Islamic territory, often wrongly translated as 'Holy War'.

jinni: jinn, supernatural being made of fire.

jund: general Arabic term for an army; largely non-elite or feudal forces by the 12th century.

kazghandah: form of mail armour for the body and arms, lined with some form of padding and usually covered in decorative cloth.

khanjar: form of large dagger or short sword, of Persian origin.

khrasani: individual from Khrasan in eastern Iran, often referring to soldiers or miners from this region.

Khwarazmshahs: dynasty of Islamic rulers originally based in Khwarazm south of the Aral Sea but subsequently controlling most of Transoxania, Iran and Afghanistan (from pre-Islamic times to 1231).

lamellar: form of armour construction in which lamels or scales are laced to each other rather than to a fabric base material.

madrasa: specialised form of mosque used for teaching.

mamluk: professional soldier of slave-recruited origin (*see* also ghulam), and subsequently the name given to a ruling dynasty in Egypt and Syria, almost invariably headed by a mamluk soldier (1252–1517).

mangonel: stone-throwing siege-machine operating on the beam-sling principle, early forms powered by a team of individuals pulling on ropes.

Manichaean-Paulicians: follower of a religious belief in which the powers of good and evil are considered equally balanced and permanently in conflict in the universe; known in Western Europe as Cathars, Albigensians, etc.

mantlet: form of large shield, usually rested on the ground to form a shield-wall or barricade.

maréchal: medieval French term for a senior official in a royal or noble household responsible for military equipment, horses and often the summoning of troops; same as marshal.

maristan: specialised form of mosque used as a hospital.

mêlée: free-for-all combat in battle, usually in the confusion following a cavalry charge.

mihrab: architectural feature in a mosque, indicating the direction of prayer towards Mecca.

mujahid: individual involved in Jihad, usually of the military form.

Murabitun, al-: Islamic ruling dynasty originating in what is now Mauritania but subsequently controlling Islamic Iberia (Andalus) and North Africa; generally known in Europe as Almoravids (1062–47 in Andalus, continued in Balearic Islands as the Banu Ghaniya until 1230/31).

mutatawi'ah: religiously motivated volunteer in an Arab-Islamic army.

Muwahhidun, al-: Islamic ruling dynasty originating in Morocco but subsequently controlling Islamic Iberia (Andalus) and North Africa, generally known in Europe as Almohades (1130–1269).

naft: Arabic term for Greek Fire and other petroleum-based incendiary weapons, also apparently applied to some very early forms of gunpowder.

Nicea: Anatolian city, capital of the main Byzantine successor state following the conquest of Constantinople by the Fourth Crusade (now called Iznik in Turkey).

pierrière: general and rather unspecific medieval French name for a stone-throwing siege-machine (*see* mangonel *above*).

pommel: front of a saddle, often raised to provide support and protection to the groin; also the large element at the end of a sword-grip.

Qahira, al-: Arabic name for Cairo, originally referred only to the Fatimid palace area or 'royal city' north of the Egyptian capital as it existed in the 10th–12th centuries.

quillons: the crosspiece or guard of a sword.

Rum: name used by Islamic peoples for that part of Anatolia conquered from the Byzantine Empire by the Seljuk Turks.

Seljuks: tribe or leading family within a confederation of Turkish tribes forming a dynasty that conquered most of the eastern Islamic world and the Middle East in the 11th century (Great Seljuk Sultanate 1040–1194; fragmented Seljuk states including the Seljuks of Rum 1048–1307 in various regions).

senechal: medieval French term for a governor or ruler's representative in a town or city.

sergeant: non-noble professional soldier, either cavalry or infantry.

Shari'a: Islamic Law based upon the Koran (Muslim Holy Book) and Hadith (sayings of the Prophet Muhammad).

Shi'a: that section of the Muslim 'umma' or community which considers that earthly authority and religious guidance (the Caliphate) rests with the descendants of the Prophet Muhammad through his daughter Fatima and his cousin 'Ali.

sufi: follower of one of many mystical 'paths' recognised by most but not all Muslims.

Sunni: that section of the Muslim 'umma' or community which considers that earthly authority and religious guidance (the Caliphate) rests with the leader accepted by the community, at first the Rashidun Caliphs (also recognised by most Shi'a), then the Umayyad Caliphs and then the 'Abbasid Caliphs).

suq al-'askar: Arab term for the mobile market which followed an army on campaign.

surcoat: cloth garment worn over armour, also used for heraldic identification purposes in Western Europe from the later 12th century.

Templar: member of the military Order of the Temple of Solomon.

Teutonic Knight: member of the military Order of the Knights of the Hospital of St Mary in Jerusalem.

troubadour: medieval Western European minstrel and poet.

turcopole: lightly equipped cavalryman in the Crusader States, often operating as a horse-archer; from a Greek term meaning 'sons of Turks'.

wazir: Arab-Islamic term for a senior government minister; Europeanised as 'vizir'.

Yasa: code of law drawn up by Genghis Khan, largely based upon Mongol tribal law and customs.

Yazidi: follower of a religion which includes elements from Judaism, Zoroastrianism, early Christian sects and Islam but denies the existence of abstract evil and accepts the transmigration of souls; sometimes wrongly called devil worshippers.

Zoroastrian: follower of a religious belief founded by Zoroaster in ancient Iran, in which the forces of good and evil are represented by Ormuzd the God of Light and Good, and Ahriman the God of Darkness and Evil; exists today as the Parsees.

Index

Figures in **bold** refer to illustrations

ACW-0997
30.0
5/14/01

DATE DUE

NOV 0 9 2001	
OCT 0 7 2003	
DEC 1 3 2010	

DEMCO, INC. 38-2931

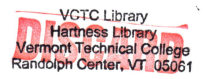